EYEWITNESS VISUAL DICTIONARIES

THE VISUAL DICTIONARY *of* SPECIAL MILITARY FORCES

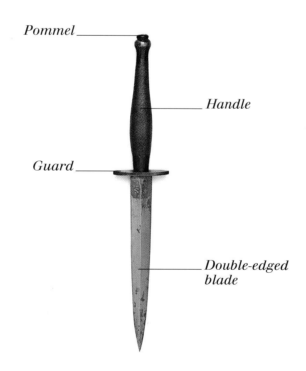

Pommel _____

_____ Handle

Guard _____

_____ Double-edged blade

BRITISH FIGHTING KNIFE, WORLD WAR II (1939-1945)

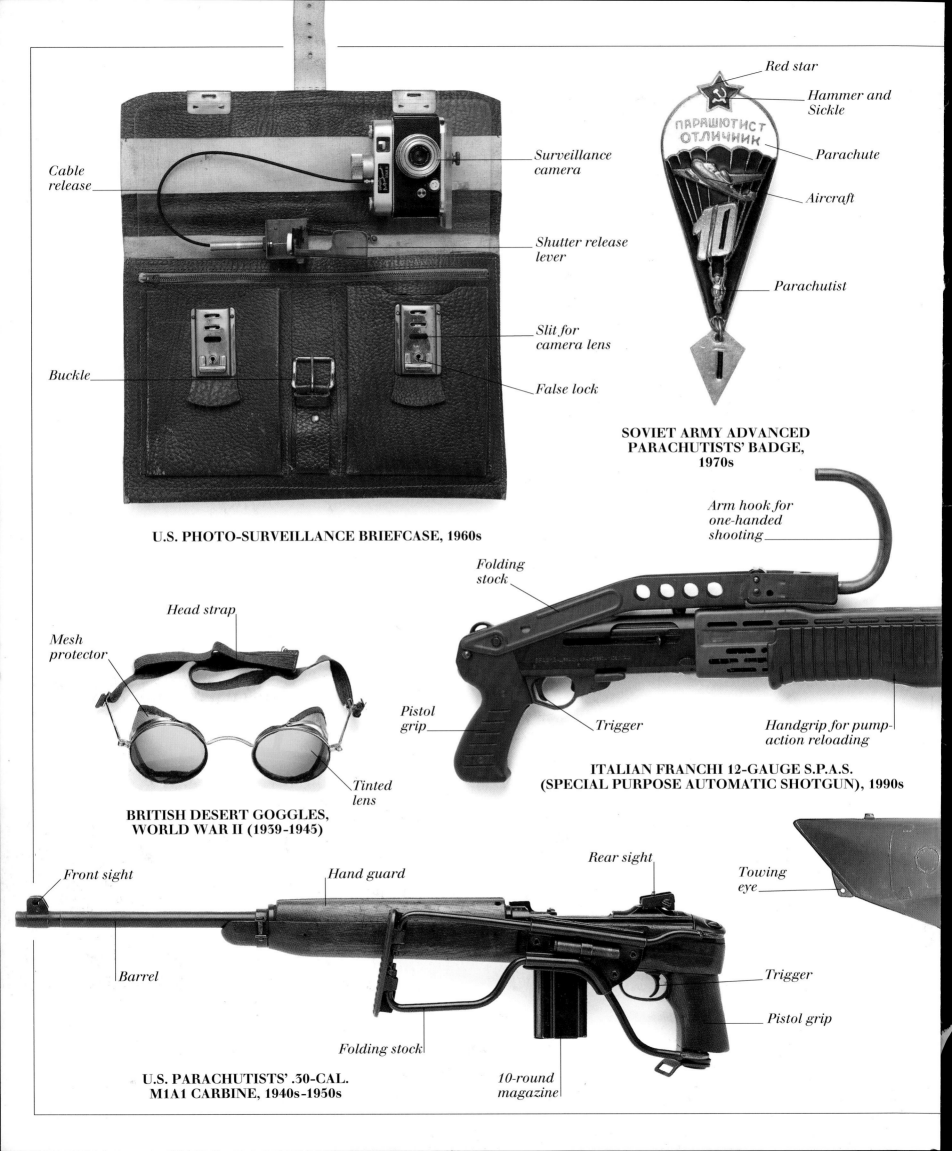

Cable release

Surveillance camera

Shutter release lever

Slit for camera lens

Buckle

False lock

U.S. PHOTO-SURVEILLANCE BRIEFCASE, 1960s

Red star

Hammer and Sickle

Parachute

ПАРАШЮТИСТ ОТЛИЧНИК

Aircraft

10

Parachutist

1

SOVIET ARMY ADVANCED PARACHUTISTS' BADGE, 1970s

Arm hook for one-handed shooting

Folding stock

Head strap

Mesh protector

Pistol grip

Trigger

Handgrip for pump-action reloading

Tinted lens

BRITISH DESERT GOGGLES, WORLD WAR II (1939-1945)

ITALIAN FRANCHI 12-GAUGE S.P.A.S. (SPECIAL PURPOSE AUTOMATIC SHOTGUN), 1990s

Front sight

Hand guard

Rear sight

Towing eye

Barrel

Trigger

Pistol grip

Folding stock

U.S. PARACHUTISTS' .30-CAL. M1A1 CARBINE, 1940s-1950s

10-round magazine

EYEWITNESS VISUAL DICTIONARIES

THE VISUAL DICTIONARY *of*
SPECIAL MILITARY FORCES

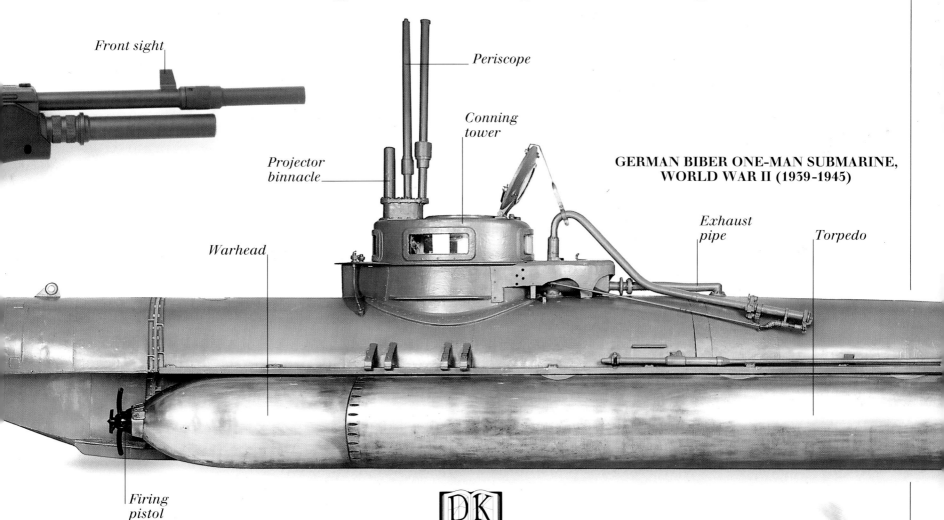

Front sight

Periscope

Conning tower

Projector binnacle

GERMAN BIBER ONE-MAN SUBMARINE, WORLD WAR II (1939-1945)

Exhaust pipe

Torpedo

Warhead

Firing pistol

DK

DORLING KINDERSLEY

LONDON • NEW YORK • STUTTGART

A DORLING KINDERSLEY BOOK

Project Art Editor Bryn Walls
Designer Paul Calver

Project Editor Louise Tucker
Consultant Editors Dr Richard Holmes, Dr John Bullen, Paul Cornish, Adrian Gilbert
U.S. Editor Charles A. Wills

Managing Art Editor Stephen Knowlden
Senior Editor Martyn Page
Managing Editor Ruth Midgley

Photography Geoff Dann, Dave Rudkin, Tim Ridley, Bruce Chisholm
Illustrations Mick Gillah, Simone End
Production Hilary Stephens

Barrel — *Pipe bowl*

Mouthpiece —

U.S. .22-CAL. PIPE PISTOL, WORLD WAR II (1939–1945)

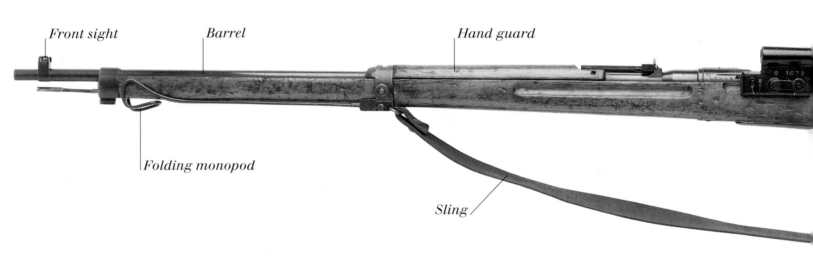

Front sight — *Barrel* — *Hand guard*

Folding monopod

Sling

First American Edition, 1993

2 4 6 8 10 9 7 5 5 1

Published in the United States by
Dorling Kindersley, Inc., 232 Madison Avenue
New York, New York 10016

Copyright © 1993 Dorling Kindersley Limited, London

Library of Congress Cataloging-in-Publication Data

Special military forces. — 1st American ed.
p. cm. — (Eyewitness visual dictionaries)
Includes index.

ISBN 1–56458–189–6
1. Special forces (Military science)—Dictionaries. I. Series.
U262.S628 1993
356'.167'03—dc20   92–53448
                                     CIP

Reproduced by Colourscan, Singapore
Printed and bound in Italy by Arnoldo Mondadori, Verona

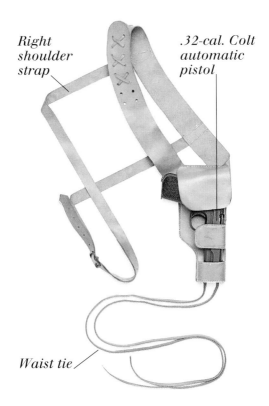

Right shoulder strap

.32-cal. Colt automatic pistol

Waist tie

BRITISH SHOULDER HOLSTER WITH AUTOMATIC PISTOL, WORLD WAR II (1939-1945)

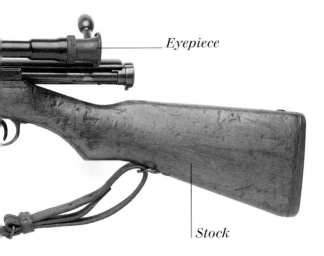

Eyepiece

Stock

JAPANESE 6.5-ᴍᴍ TYPE 97 SNIPER'S RIFLE, c.1937

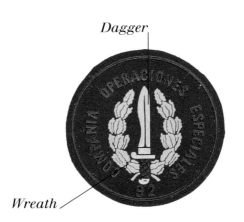

Dagger

Wreath

SPANISH ARMY SPECIAL FORCES' BADGE, 1990s

Contents

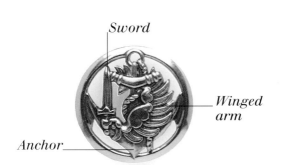

Sword

Winged arm

Anchor

FRENCH MARINE PARACHUTISTS' BADGE, 1970s

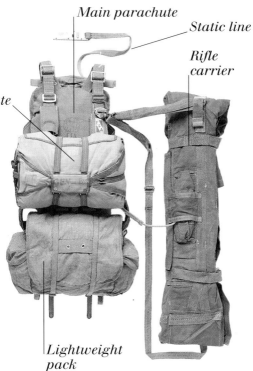

Main parachute

Static line

Rifle carrier

Reserve parachute

Lightweight pack

FRENCH PARACHUTISTS' EQUIPMENT, 1970s

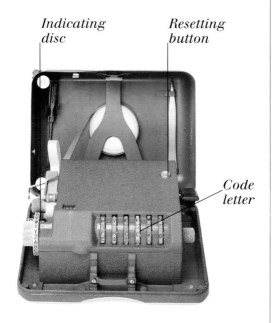

Indicating disc

Resetting button

Code letter

U.S. M-209-B CIPHER MACHINE, WORLD WAR II (1939-1945)

Military intelligence

MILITARY INTELLIGENCE INVOLVES GATHERING and analyzing information that may be helpful in planning military operations. Intelligence may be collected from many sources, including secret documents obtained by agents working for intelligence agencies, aerial photographs taken by reconnaissance aircraft, and even postcards and photographs of enemy territory sent in by the general public. During World War II, military intelligence provided information for the Allies to begin the liberation of German-occupied Europe in the D-Day landings on the Normandy coastline of France. Aerial photographs showed the exact positions of the German troops and of the obstacles they had placed on the beaches to prevent a seaborne invasion. Using these photographs, together with maps and other information, detailed briefing models of the landing areas on the Normandy beaches were made so that the Allied commanders were familiar with the area before launching their troops.

POSTCARDS OF NORMANDY, FRANCE, 1930s–1940s

Mouth of River Orne

Ouistreham

MAP OF "SWORD" BEACH D-DAY LANDING AREA, NORMANDY, FRANCE, APRIL 1944

"Sword," the code name for one of five beaches designated by the Allies for the D-Day landings

"Queen," the code name for a section of "Sword" beach

"Top secret," indicating classified information

"White," the code name for a subsection of beach

Warning that underwater obstacles were being laid by the Germans

Sea

Line designating subdivision of beaches

Coastline

River Orne

Beach

La Brèche

Ouistreham

MAP OF OUISTREHAM AREA OF "SWORD" BEACH, NORMANDY, FRANCE, MAY 1944

Key to map symbols

Scale bar

Key to map symbols

Owner of map (Lieutenant D. Holman)

Note about sea levels

Note about channels and sandbanks

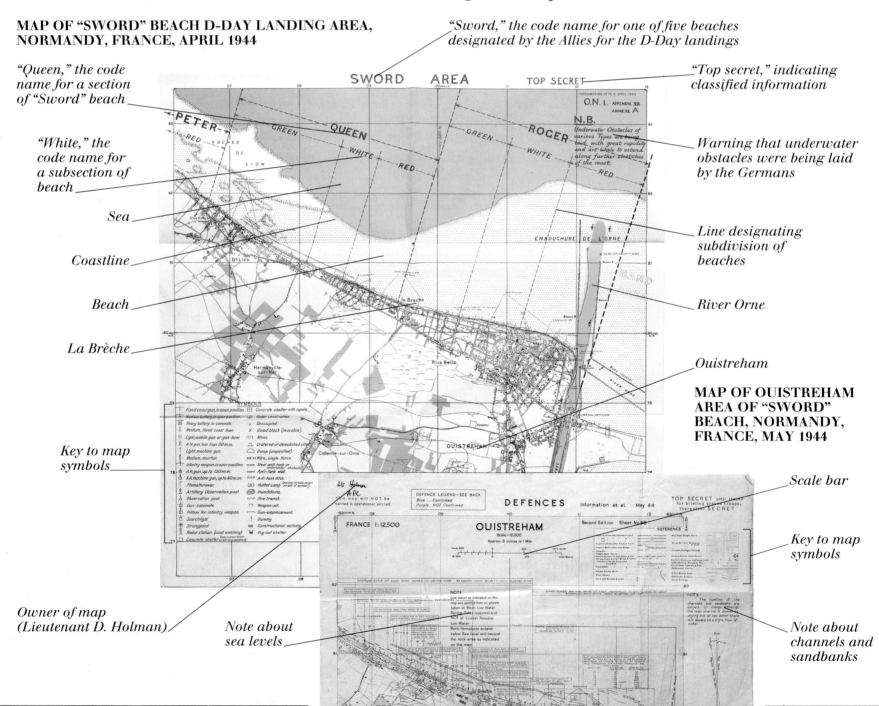

COMPOSITE PANORAMA OF COASTLINE OF "SWORD" BEACH, NORMANDY, FRANCE, 1944

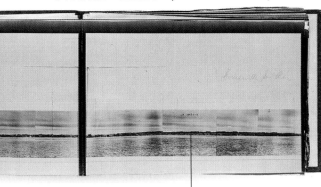

La Brèche

AERIAL PHOTOGRAPHS OF COASTLINE OF FRANCE, MARCH–MAY 1944

Inland France

Road

Fields

Buildings

Beach

Sea

HIGH-LEVEL OVERHEAD AERIAL PHOTOGRAPH

Jagged steel obstacles ("hedgehogs")

Beach

Stakes driven into beach

Sea

Marks made by intelligence officers to indicate where Germans may place mines

LOW-LEVEL OBLIQUE AERIAL PHOTOGRAPH

BRIEFING MODEL OF SECTION OF D-DAY LANDING BEACH, NORMANDY, FRANCE, 1944

Beach

Road

Minefield (unconfirmed)

Label indicating that the windows of buildings are bricked up in this area, showing that an invasion may have been expected here

Label indicating seawall

Label indicating seawall

Designated beach sector

Label indicating gaps in seawall

Label indicating houses that have been fortified by the Germans

Code for subdivision of beach into "red" area

Code for subdivision of beach into "white" area

Sea

Anti-tank ditch

Building

Wood

Minefield

Minefield

Railroad

SEA WALL

GAPS

SEA WALL

WINDOWS BRICKED UP

FORTIFIED HOUSES

Wartime secret agents 1

DURING WORLD WAR II, hundreds of secret agents were parachuted behind enemy lines to support and coordinate local resistance groups. The British SOE (Special Operations Executive) and the American OSS (Office of Strategic Services) were established to train and equip the agents selected for such missions. Aircraft carrying the agents and their equipment were guided to safe dropping zones by another agent on the ground, who communicated with the pilot using a portable transceiver, such as the S-phone. Other transceivers, often disguised as suitcases, were used to maintain contact with home base (see pp. 10-11). When they went on secret missions, agents were often armed with silent weapons, such as knives or silenced pistols. Agents were also equipped with escape aids, such as compasses and maps, for use if they were in danger of being captured and had to flee. These items were usually hidden in secret compartments in various everyday objects, such as cigarette lighters and fountain pens (see pp. 12-13).

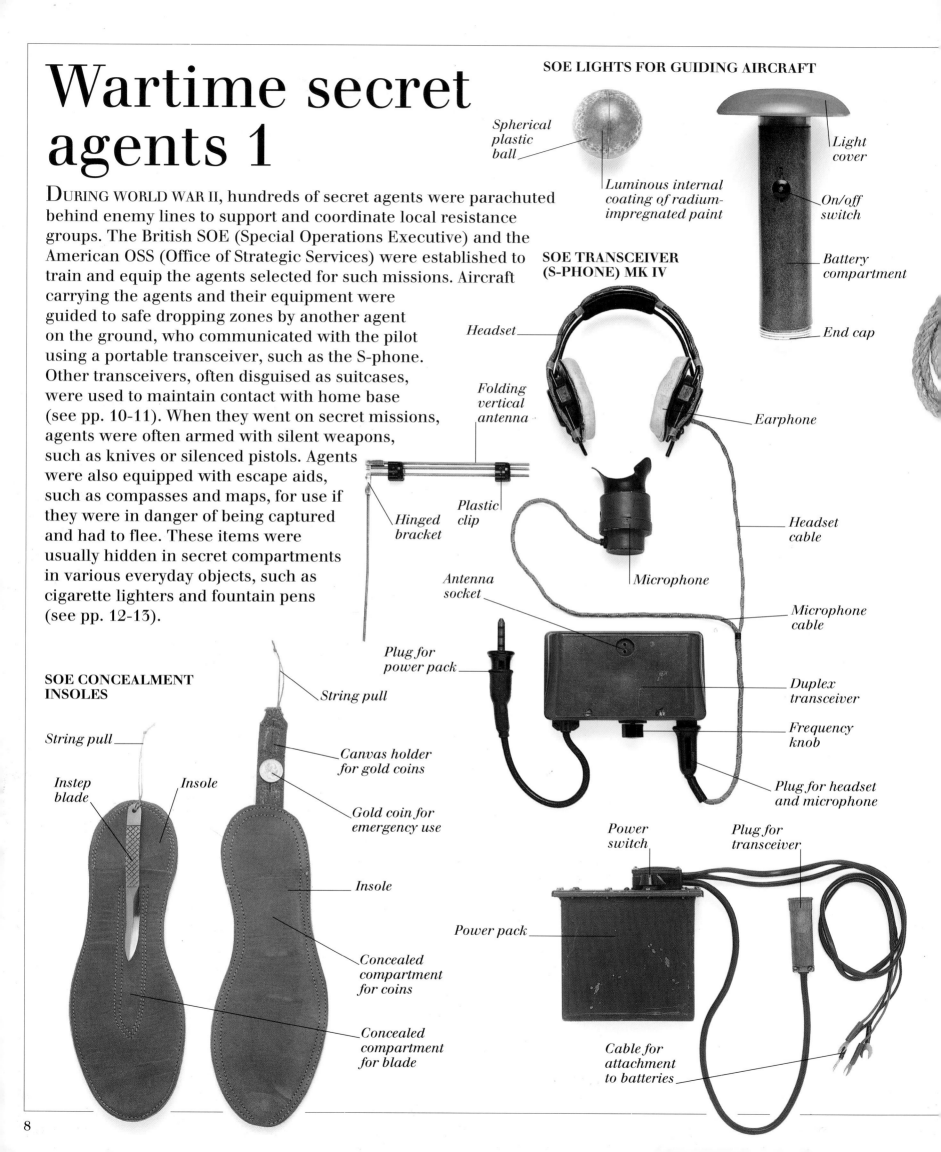

Spherical plastic ball

Luminous internal coating of radium-impregnated paint

Light cover

On/off switch

Battery compartment

End cap

SOE TRANSCEIVER (S-PHONE) MK IV

Headset

Folding vertical antenna

Hinged bracket

Plastic clip

Earphone

Headset cable

Antenna socket

Microphone

Microphone cable

Plug for power pack

Duplex transceiver

Frequency knob

Plug for headset and microphone

Power switch

Plug for transceiver

Power pack

Cable for attachment to batteries

SOE CONCEALMENT INSOLES

String pull

String pull

Canvas holder for gold coins

Instep blade

Insole

Gold coin for emergency use

Insole

Concealed compartment for coins

Concealed compartment for blade

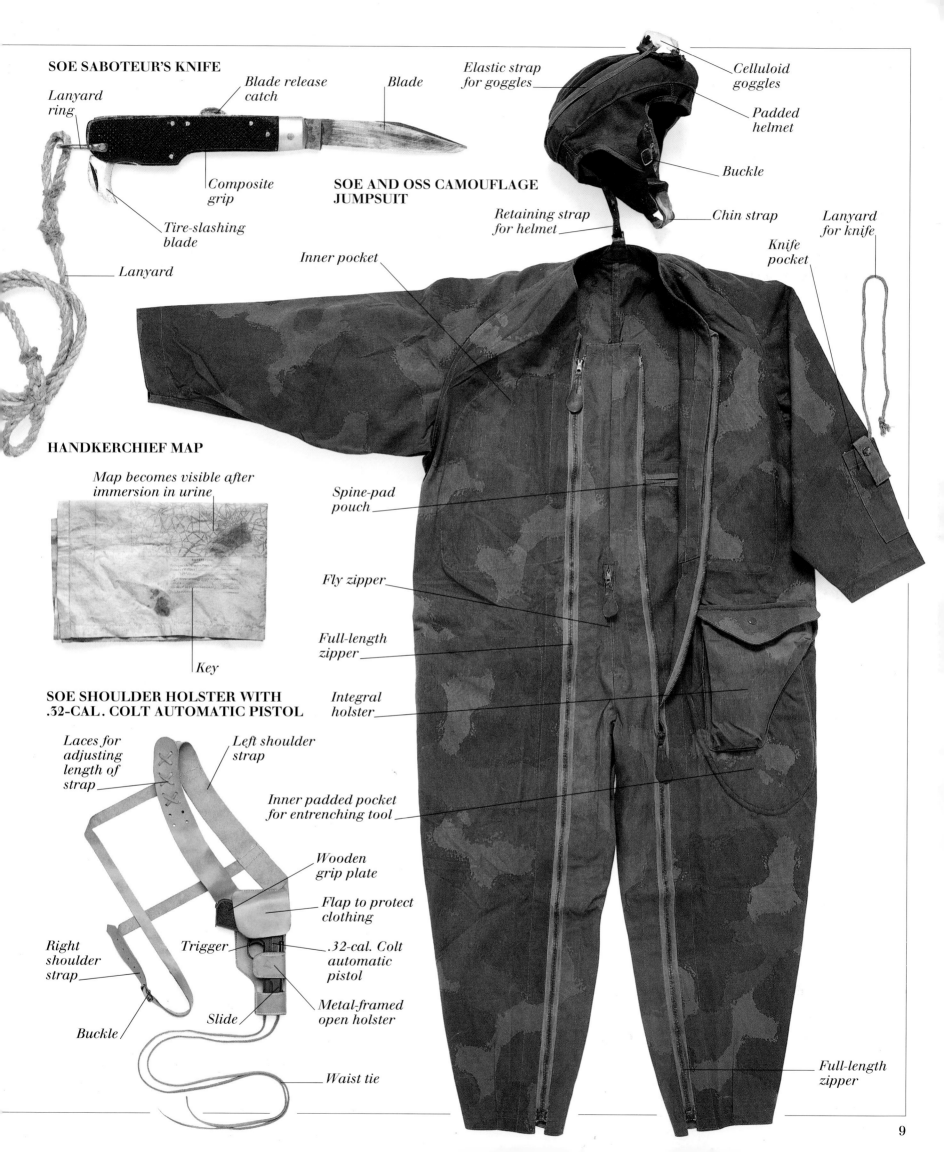

SOE SABOTEUR'S KNIFE

Lanyard ring

Blade release catch

Blade

Composite grip

Tire-slashing blade

Lanyard

SOE AND OSS CAMOUFLAGE JUMPSUIT

Elastic strap for goggles

Celluloid goggles

Padded helmet

Buckle

Retaining strap for helmet

Chin strap

Lanyard for knife

Inner pocket

Knife pocket

HANDKERCHIEF MAP

Map becomes visible after immersion in urine

Spine-pad pouch

Fly zipper

Full-length zipper

Key

Integral holster

SOE SHOULDER HOLSTER WITH .32-CAL. COLT AUTOMATIC PISTOL

Inner padded pocket for entrenching tool

Laces for adjusting length of strap

Left shoulder strap

Wooden grip plate

Flap to protect clothing

Right shoulder strap

Trigger

.32-cal. Colt automatic pistol

Slide

Metal-framed open holster

Buckle

Waist tie

Full-length zipper

Wartime secret agents 2

SOE AND OSS SPECIAL FORCES' BADGE

Initials of Special Forces

Wing

OSS "BEANO" GRENADE

Secondary arming mechanism and fuse

Primary safety ring

Grenade body

GRENADE T 13
AMM. LOT

FALSE GERMAN IDENTIFICATION DOCUMENT MADE BY OSS

Place of issue

Identification number

Expiration date

Surname

Forenames

Date of birth

Place of birth

Profession (lawyer)

Unalterable distinguishing marks (none)

Notes (none)

Alterable distinguishing marks (none)

Forged imprint of German national emblem

Forged imprint of Berlin police chief

Photograph of General William J. Donovan (Director of the OSS)

Kennort: *Berlin*
Kennnummer: *A 390962*
Gültig bis *22. Mai* 19*45*
Name *Donovan*
Vornamen *William Joseph*
Geburtstag *1. Januar 1883*
Geburtsort *Buffalo N.Y.*
Beruf *Rechtsanwalt*
Unveränderliche Kennzeichen *fehlen*
Veränderliche Kennzeichen *fehlen*
Bemerkungen: *Keine*

(Unterschrift des Kennkarteninhabers)

Berlin, den *22. Mai* 19*40*

Der Polizeipräsident in Berlin

(Unterschrift des ausfertigenden Beamten)

Front sight

Suppressor (silencer) end cap

OSS CLANDESTINE BLADE KIT

Single-hook thrust dagger

Hatpin dagger

Triple-edged concealment dagger

Manufacturer's plate

Open-handled dagger

Ring dagger

OSS marking

Thumb knife

Triple-edged dart

Folding leather case

Double-edged knife

Blackened double-edged knife

Lapel knife

Lacing for case

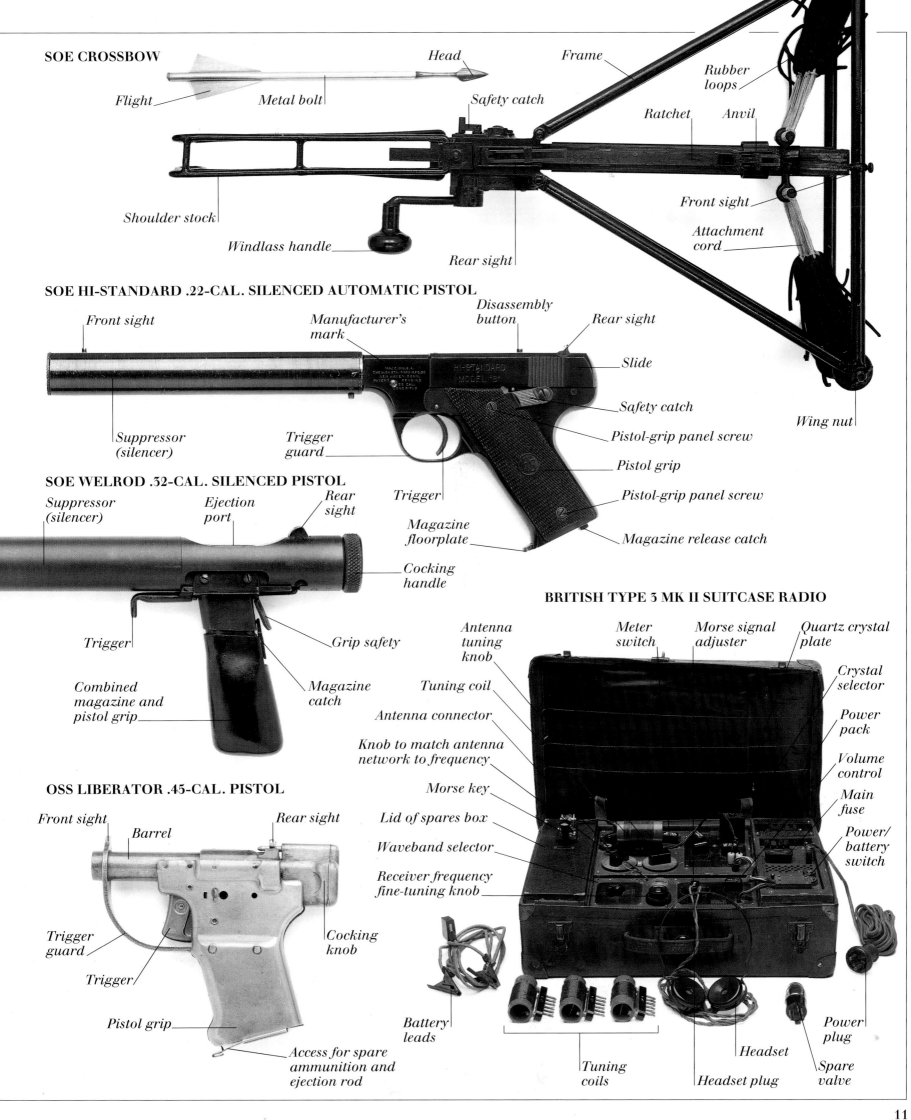

SOE CROSSBOW

Flight
Metal bolt
Head
Frame
Rubber loops
Safety catch
Ratchet
Anvil
Shoulder stock
Front sight
Windlass handle
Attachment cord
Rear sight

SOE HI-STANDARD .22-CAL. SILENCED AUTOMATIC PISTOL

Front sight
Manufacturer's mark
Disassembly button
Rear sight
Slide
Safety catch
Suppressor (silencer)
Trigger guard
Pistol-grip panel screw
Pistol grip
Trigger
Pistol-grip panel screw
Magazine floorplate
Magazine release catch
Wing nut

SOE WELROD .32-CAL. SILENCED PISTOL

Suppressor (silencer)
Ejection port
Rear sight
Cocking handle
Trigger
Grip safety
Combined magazine and pistol grip
Magazine catch

BRITISH TYPE 3 MK II SUITCASE RADIO

Antenna tuning knob
Meter switch
Morse signal adjuster
Quartz crystal plate
Tuning coil
Crystal selector
Antenna connector
Power pack
Knob to match antenna network to frequency
Volume control
Morse key
Main fuse
Lid of spares box
Power/ battery switch
Waveband selector
Receiver frequency fine-tuning knob

OSS LIBERATOR .45-CAL. PISTOL

Front sight
Rear sight
Barrel
Trigger guard
Cocking knob
Trigger
Pistol grip
Battery leads
Access for spare ammunition and ejection rod
Tuning coils
Headset
Headset plug
Power plug
Spare valve

Wartime secret agents 3

SHAVING BRUSH WITH CONCEALED COMPARTMENT

Bristles

Tissue map wrapped in cloth

CIGARETTE LIGHTER WITH CONCEALED COMPASS

Striker

Wick

Grip

Screw thread

Tie

DICE SHAKER WITH CONCEALED COMPARTMENT

Top of sectioned compartment

Red spot indicates north

Attachment ring

Top cap

Compass

Attachment chain

Concealed compartment

Hollow handle

Lighter fuel compartment

Screw

Compartment for spare flint

Dice shaker

Red spot indicates north

Base cap

HAIRBRUSH WITH CONCEALED COMPARTMENT

Compartment for compass needle

False top for compass compartment with reverse-thread screw

Compass

Base of hairbrush

PLAYING CARDS WITH CONCEALED MAP SECTIONS

Compartment for compass

Concealed compartment

Card's surface turned back

Bristles

Top of hairbrush

8

Playing card

Section of map

Numbered section of map

FOUNTAIN PEN WITH CONCEALED MAP AND COMPASS

Map concealed in barrel

Ink filling lever

Compass

Base cap

End points north when clip is pivoted

Magnetized pen clip

Mushroom-headed cap

BUCKLE COMPASS

Magnetic pointer

Clasp

End points north when nib is pivoted

MAGNETIZED PEN NIB

Pivot hole

End points north

Pivot

Pipe bowl containing map hidden in asbestos lining

MATCH CONTAINING MAGNETIZED NEEDLE

Wood concealing magnetized needle

Head of match points north when match is floated

PIPE WITH CONCEALED ITEMS

Mouthpiece

Stopper

Concealed container

Screw thread

Compass

Wadding

Hole for smoke to pass through

Smoke passage

LEATHER BOOTHEEL WITH CONCEALED COMPARTMENT

ITEMS CONTAINED IN HAIRBRUSH

Red spot indicates north

Compass needle

Miniature compass

Pivot hole

North indicator

Concealed compartment

Miniature saw

RUBBER BOOTHEEL WITH CONCEALED COMPARTMENT

Concealed compartment

Serrated edge

Tissue map

Secret message

Concealed weapons

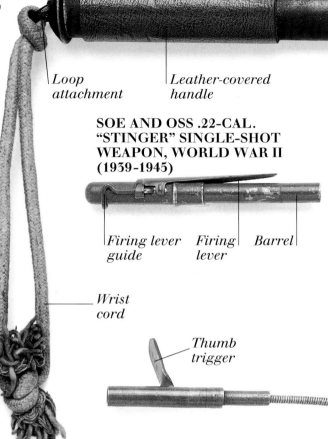

Loop attachment

Leather-covered handle

SECRET AGENTS OPERATING inside enemy territory may carry concealed weapons, mainly for use as a last resort to avoid capture. During World War II, many such weapons were designed specifically for agents of the British SOE (Special Operations Executive) and American OSS (Office of Strategic Services). Agents required weapons that were small enough to be hidden easily or disguised as everyday objects. Because these weapons were so small, they had a limited range – only 12 ft (3.7 m) for some of the pistols shown here. Some weapons could be concealed in clothing. Such weapons ranged from a simple lapel knife to the more sophisticated belt pistol.

FRENCH FIVE-SHOT RING REVOLVER, 1870s

SOE AND OSS .22-CAL. "STINGER" SINGLE-SHOT WEAPON, WORLD WAR II (1939-1945)

Firing lever guide   *Firing lever*   *Barrel*

Wrist cord

Thumb trigger

OSS .22-CAL. PIPE PISTOL, WORLD WAR II (1939-1945)

Pipe bowl

Mouthpiece   *Barrel*

SOE LAPEL KNIFE, WORLD WAR II (1939-1945)

Thumb grip   *Double-edged blade*

Trigger bar   *Extractor*
Sear   *Ejection port*   *Slide*
Shortened barrel

BRITISH SPECIAL FORCES' BELT PISTOL, WORLD WAR II (1939-1945)

Hammer

Breech return lever

Recoil spring

Trigger guard

Trigger

Modified Webley & Scott 6.35-mm pistol

Leather scabbard

Patch for attachment to lapel

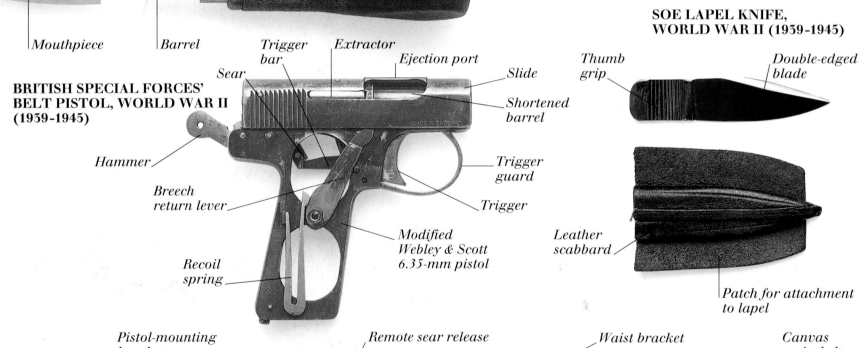

Pistol-mounting bracket   *Remote sear release*   *Waist bracket*   *Canvas waist belt*

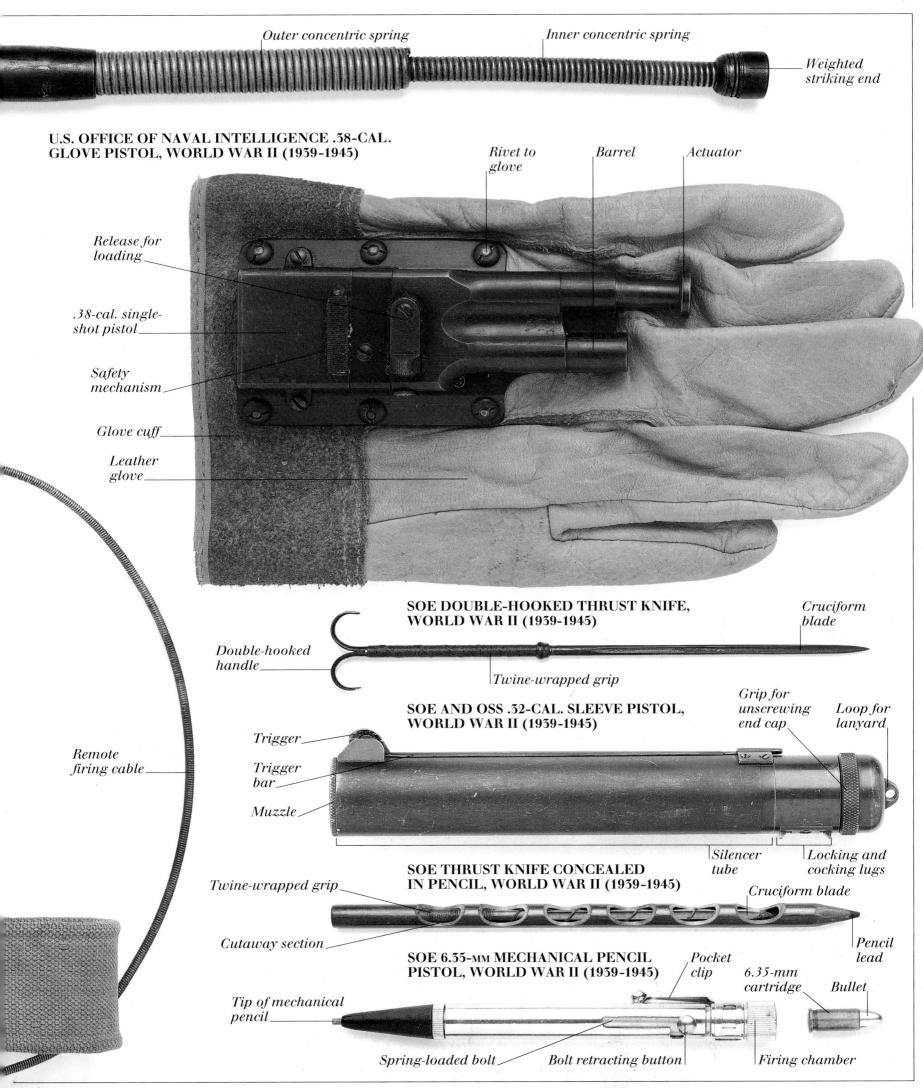

Outer concentric spring

Inner concentric spring

Weighted striking end

U.S. OFFICE OF NAVAL INTELLIGENCE .38-CAL. GLOVE PISTOL, WORLD WAR II (1939-1945)

Rivet to glove

Barrel

Actuator

Release for loading

.38-cal. single-shot pistol

Safety mechanism

Glove cuff

Leather glove

SOE DOUBLE-HOOKED THRUST KNIFE, WORLD WAR II (1939-1945)

Cruciform blade

Double-hooked handle

Twine-wrapped grip

SOE AND OSS .32-CAL. SLEEVE PISTOL, WORLD WAR II (1939-1945)

Grip for unscrewing end cap

Loop for lanyard

Remote firing cable

Trigger

Trigger bar

Muzzle

Silencer tube

Locking and cocking lugs

SOE THRUST KNIFE CONCEALED IN PENCIL, WORLD WAR II (1939-1945)

Twine-wrapped grip

Cruciform blade

Cutaway section

Pencil lead

SOE 6.35-ᴍᴍ MECHANICAL PENCIL PISTOL, WORLD WAR II (1939-1945)

Pocket clip

6.35-mm cartridge

Bullet

Tip of mechanical pencil

Spring-loaded bolt

Bolt retracting button

Firing chamber

Desert forces

ARMED FORCES OPERATING IN THE DESERT have to cope with extremes of temperature and water shortage, as well as facing the difficulties of defending and traveling across vast areas of almost featureless terrain. Some forces, such as the French Foreign Legion, have become specialists in desert warfare. Other nations established units specifically to carry out reconnaissance and sabotage in the desert; such units included the British Long Range Desert Group and the SAS (Special Air Service). Reliable four-wheel-drive vehicles – such as the modified Land Rover shown here – are essential in the desert. This vehicle (known as the "Pink Panther" because of the color of its sand camouflage) was fitted with large-capacity fuel tanks to give it a longer than average range of about 1,500 miles (2,400 km).

BRITISH SUN COMPASS, WORLD WAR II (1939-1945)

Time calibration scale

Instructions

360° calibrations

Gnomon

Shadow marker

Latitude calibrations
(red figures for southern
latitudes, black figures
for northern latitudes)

Latitude plate

Base
plate

Adjustment slot
for latitude plate

Spirit level

**SIDE VIEW OF BRITISH SPECIAL AIR SERVICE'S
LAND ROVER ("PINK PANTHER"), 1960s-1980s**

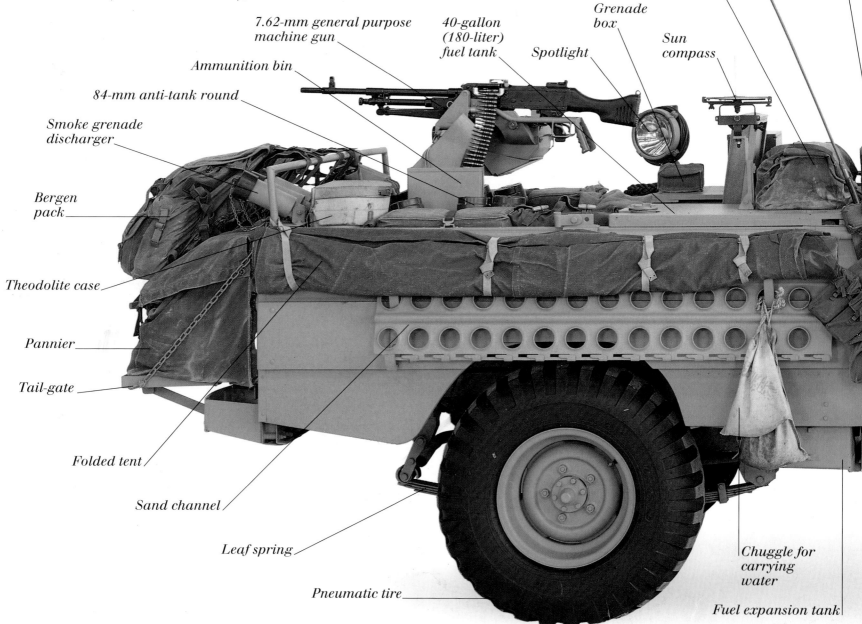

VHF radio antenna

UHF radio

84-mm anti-tank
weapon stowage

Grenade
box

7.62-mm general purpose
machine gun

40-gallon
(180-liter)
fuel tank

Sun
compass

Spotlight

Ammunition bin

84-mm anti-tank round

Smoke grenade
discharger

Bergen
pack

Theodolite case

Pannier

Tail-gate

Folded tent

Sand channel

Leaf spring

Pneumatic tire

Chuggle for
carrying
water

Fuel expansion tank

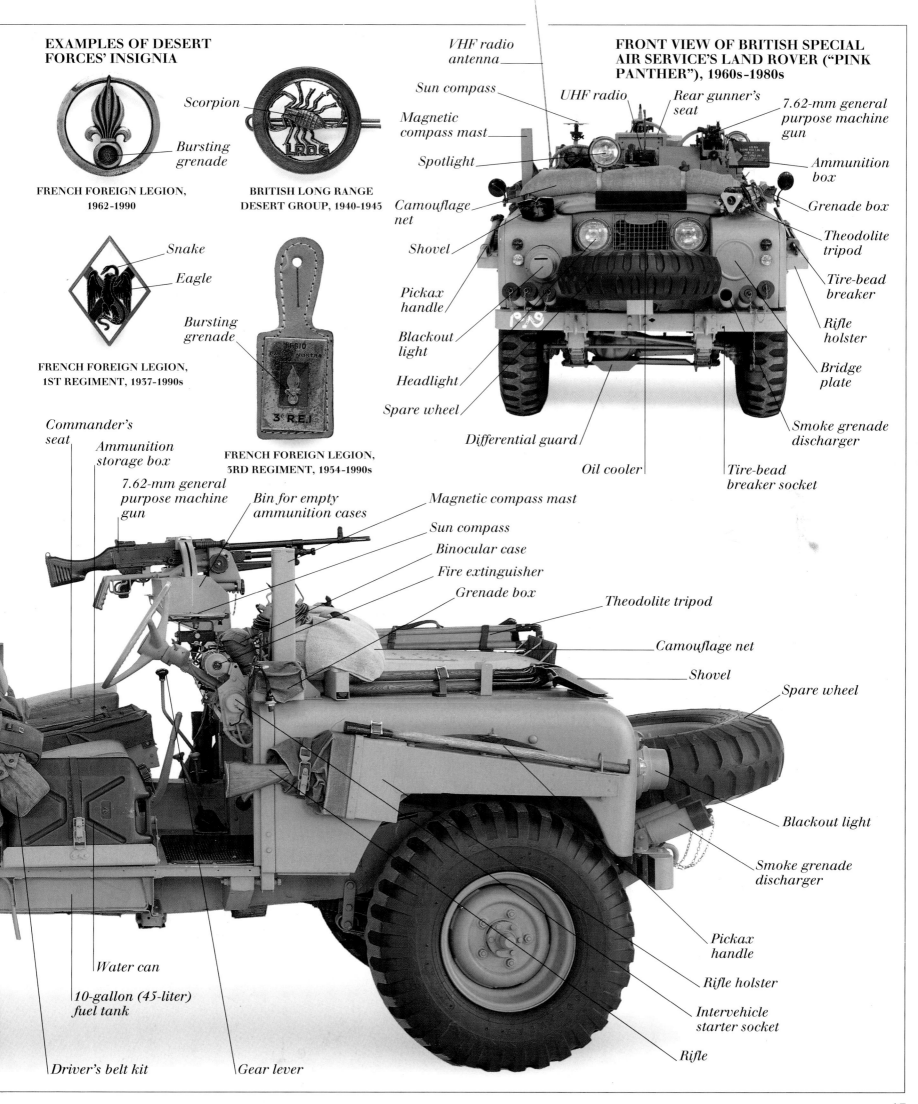

EXAMPLES OF DESERT FORCES' INSIGNIA

Scorpion

Bursting grenade

FRENCH FOREIGN LEGION, 1962-1990

BRITISH LONG RANGE DESERT GROUP, 1940-1945

Snake

Eagle

FRENCH FOREIGN LEGION, 1ST REGIMENT, 1937-1990s

Bursting grenade

FRENCH FOREIGN LEGION, 3RD REGIMENT, 1954-1990s

FRONT VIEW OF BRITISH SPECIAL AIR SERVICE'S LAND ROVER ("PINK PANTHER"), 1960s-1980s

VHF radio antenna

Sun compass

UHF radio

Rear gunner's seat

7.62-mm general purpose machine gun

Magnetic compass mast

Spotlight

Ammunition box

Camouflage net

Grenade box

Shovel

Theodolite tripod

Pickax handle

Tire-bead breaker

Blackout light

Rifle holster

Headlight

Bridge plate

Spare wheel

Differential guard

Smoke grenade discharger

Oil cooler

Tire-bead breaker socket

Commander's seat

Ammunition storage box

7.62-mm general purpose machine gun

Bin for empty ammunition cases

Magnetic compass mast

Sun compass

Binocular case

Fire extinguisher

Grenade box

Theodolite tripod

Camouflage net

Shovel

Spare wheel

Blackout light

Smoke grenade discharger

Pickax handle

Water can

Rifle holster

10-gallon (45-liter) fuel tank

Intervehicle starter socket

Driver's belt kit

Gear lever

Rifle

Covert amphibious forces

COVERT AMPHIBIOUS forces not only have to be expert at fighting on land and at sea, but they must also be skilled at carrying out operations in the greatest secrecy. Their missions range from reconnaissance to attacks on enemy ships and harbor defenses. Because of the clandestine nature of their operations, covert amphibious forces often use silent boats such as canoes. During World War II, a special submersible craft was invented. Known as the "Sleeping Beauty," this vessel could function both as a canoe and as a mini-submarine. Despite its versatility, however, the Sleeping Beauty was not widely used. Acts of sabotage carried out by covert amphibious forces often involve disabling enemy ships, typically by attaching limpet mines to the hulls. Various timing devices have been used to detonate such mines, including acetone time-delay fuses, which employ different concentrations of acetone to vary the length of time before the mine is detonated.

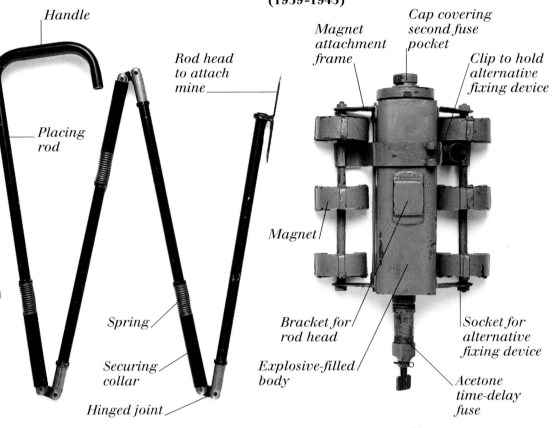

BRITISH LIMPET MINE AND PLACING ROD, WORLD WAR II (1939-1945)

Handle

Rod head to attach mine

Placing rod

Spring

Securing collar

Hinged joint

Cap covering second fuse pocket

Magnet attachment frame

Clip to hold alternative fixing device

Magnet

Bracket for rod head

Explosive-filled body

Socket for alternative fixing device

Acetone time-delay fuse

BRITISH WATERPROOF FLASHLIGHT, WORLD WAR II (1939-1945)

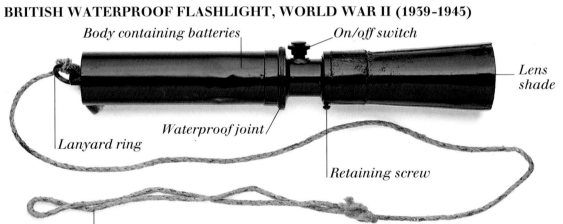

Body containing batteries

On/off switch

Lens shade

Lanyard ring

Waterproof joint

Retaining screw

Lanyard

BRITISH MOTORIZED SUBMERSIBLE CANOE ("SLEEPING BEAUTY"), WORLD WAR II (1939-1945)

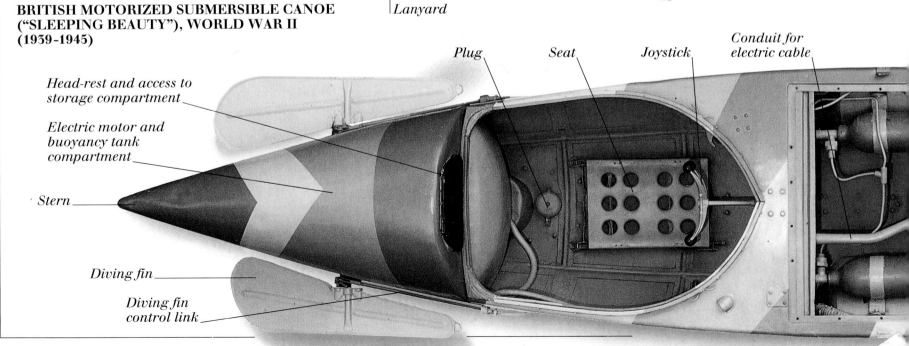

Plug

Seat

Joystick

Conduit for electric cable

Head-rest and access to storage compartment

Electric motor and buoyancy tank compartment

Stern

Diving fin

Diving fin control link

BRITISH ACETONE TIME-DELAY FUSE, WORLD WAR II (1939-1945)

U.S. INGRAM 9-MM MAC 10 SUBMACHINE GUN, 1970s–1990s

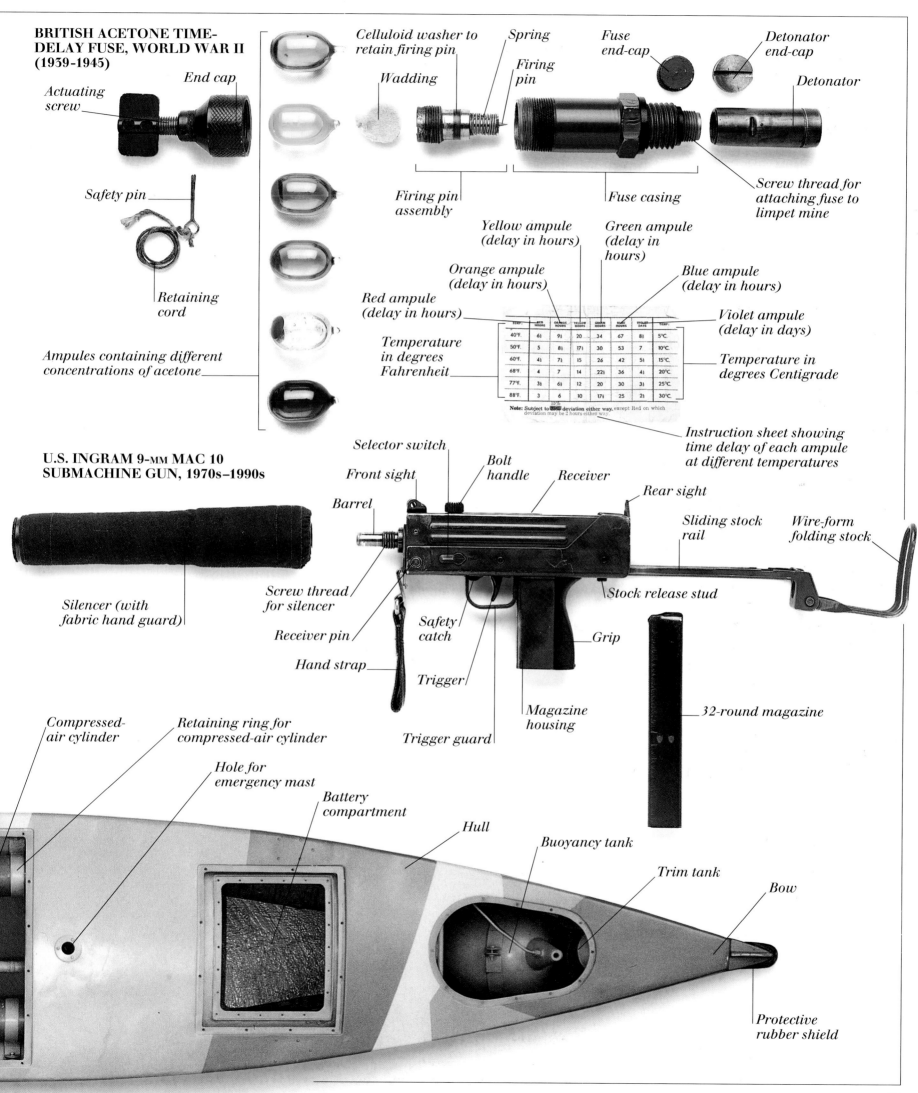

Actuating screw

End cap

Celluloid washer to retain firing pin

Wadding

Spring

Firing pin

Fuse end-cap

Detonator end-cap

Detonator

Safety pin

Firing pin assembly

Fuse casing

Screw thread for attaching fuse to limpet mine

Retaining cord

Yellow ampule (delay in hours)

Green ampule (delay in hours)

Orange ampule (delay in hours)

Blue ampule (delay in hours)

Red ampule (delay in hours)

Violet ampule (delay in days)

Temperature in degrees Fahrenheit

Temperature in degrees Centigrade

Ampules containing different concentrations of acetone

TEMP.	RED HOURS	ORANGE HOURS	YELLOW HOURS	GREEN HOURS	BLUE HOURS	VIOLET DAYS	TEMP.
40°F.	6½	9½	20	34	67	8½	5°C.
50°F.	5	8½	17½	30	53	7	10°C.
60°F.	4½	7½	15	26	42	5½	15°C.
68°F.	4	7	14	22½	36	4½	20°C.
77°F.	3½	6½	12	20	30	3½	25°C.
88°F.	3	6	10	17½	25	2½	30°C.

Note: Subject to 15% deviation either way, except Red on which deviation may be 2 hours either way.

Instruction sheet showing time delay of each ampule at different temperatures

Selector switch

Bolt handle

Front sight

Receiver

Rear sight

Barrel

Sliding stock rail

Wire-form folding stock

Silencer (with fabric hand guard)

Screw thread for silencer

Receiver pin

Safety catch

Stock release stud

Grip

Hand strap

Trigger

Magazine housing

32-round magazine

Trigger guard

Compressed-air cylinder

Retaining ring for compressed-air cylinder

Hole for emergency mast

Battery compartment

Hull

Buoyancy tank

Trim tank

Bow

Protective rubber shield

Marines

FRENCH MARINE PARACHUTISTS' BADGE, 1970s

MARINES ARE TROOPS WHOSE PRIMARY TASK is to carry out amphibious (ship-to-shore) landings and establish beachheads on enemy territory. Most of the missions that marines undertake require special craft to transport them ashore. There are various types of such craft, and the type used depends on the situation. For secretly carrying small groups ashore, a fast, maneuverable, unarmored boat may be used, such as the "Rigid Raider." For landing larger groups while under enemy fire, a heavy-duty amphibious vehicle is more suitable, such as the LVTP-7 Amtrac. This vehicle is launched from a ship and can carry 25 marines ashore in relative safety because it is armored, as well as being armed with a machine gun and smoke-grenade dischargers.

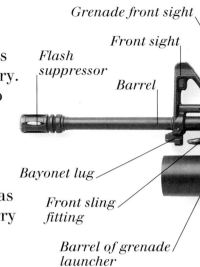

Grenade front sight
Front sight
Flash suppressor
Barrel
Bayonet lug
Front sling fitting
Barrel of grenade launcher

BRITISH "RIGID RAIDER," 1980s-1990s

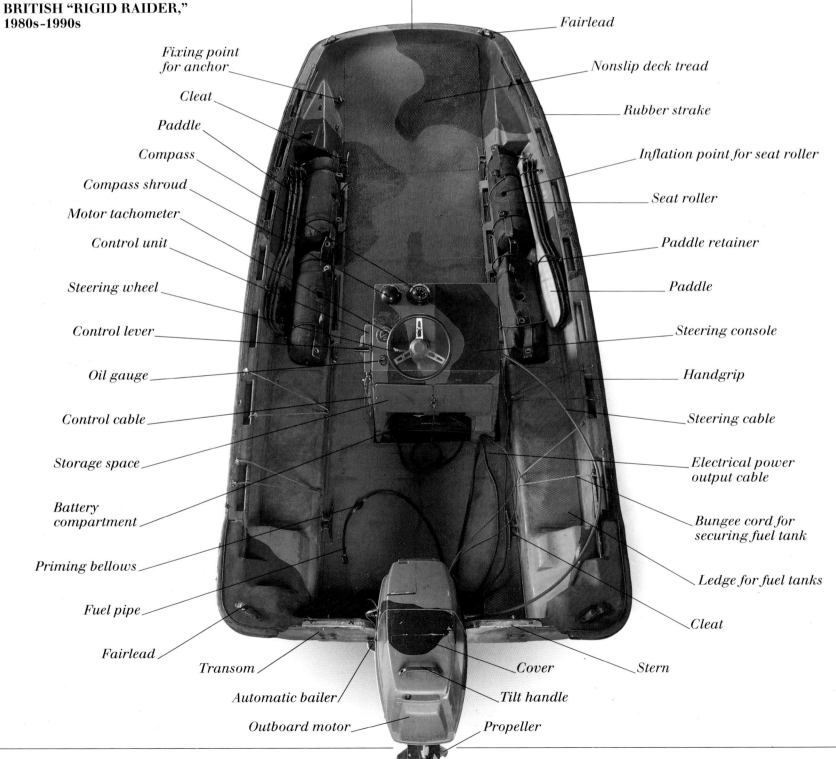

Bow
Fairlead
Fixing point for anchor
Nonslip deck tread
Cleat
Rubber strake
Paddle
Compass
Inflation point for seat roller
Compass shroud
Seat roller
Motor tachometer
Control unit
Paddle retainer
Steering wheel
Paddle
Control lever
Steering console
Oil gauge
Handgrip
Control cable
Steering cable
Storage space
Electrical power output cable
Battery compartment
Bungee cord for securing fuel tank
Priming bellows
Ledge for fuel tanks
Fuel pipe
Cleat
Fairlead
Transom
Cover
Stern
Automatic bailer
Tilt handle
Outboard motor
Propeller

20

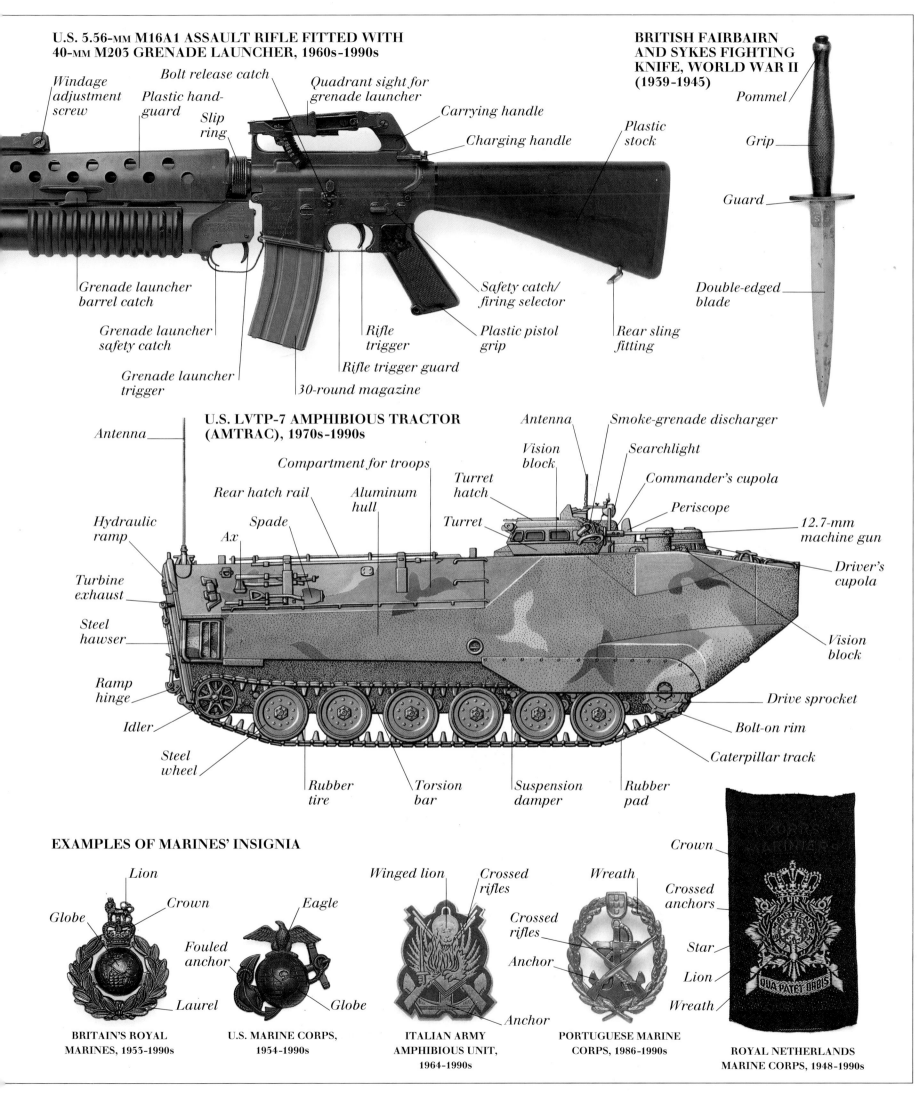

U.S. 5.56-MM M16A1 ASSAULT RIFLE FITTED WITH 40-MM M203 GRENADE LAUNCHER, 1960s–1990s

Windage adjustment screw

Bolt release catch

Plastic hand-guard

Quadrant sight for grenade launcher

Slip ring

Carrying handle

Charging handle

Plastic stock

Grenade launcher barrel catch

Grenade launcher safety catch

Grenade launcher trigger

Rifle trigger

Rifle trigger guard

30-round magazine

Safety catch/firing selector

Plastic pistol grip

Rear sling fitting

BRITISH FAIRBAIRN AND SYKES FIGHTING KNIFE, WORLD WAR II (1939–1945)

Pommel

Grip

Guard

Double-edged blade

U.S. LVTP-7 AMPHIBIOUS TRACTOR (AMTRAC), 1970s–1990s

Antenna

Compartment for troops

Rear hatch rail

Aluminum hull

Spade

Ax

Hydraulic ramp

Turbine exhaust

Steel hawser

Ramp hinge

Idler

Steel wheel

Rubber tire

Torsion bar

Suspension damper

Rubber pad

Antenna

Smoke-grenade discharger

Vision block

Searchlight

Turret hatch

Commander's cupola

Turret

Periscope

12.7-mm machine gun

Driver's cupola

Vision block

Drive sprocket

Bolt-on rim

Caterpillar track

EXAMPLES OF MARINES' INSIGNIA

Lion

Crown

Globe

Fouled anchor

Laurel

Globe

Eagle

Winged lion

Crossed rifles

Crossed rifles

Anchor

Anchor

Wreath

Crossed rifles

Anchor

Crown

Crossed anchors

Star

Lion

Wreath

BRITAIN'S ROYAL MARINES, 1953–1990s

U.S. MARINE CORPS, 1954–1990s

ITALIAN ARMY AMPHIBIOUS UNIT, 1964–1990s

PORTUGUESE MARINE CORPS, 1986–1990s

ROYAL NETHERLANDS MARINE CORPS, 1948–1990s

Undersea forces

UNDERSEA FORCES ARE SPECIALLY TRAINED to perform underwater naval operations. During World War II, various submersibles were invented to secretly penetrate enemy harbor defenses. The Italians produced the Maiale ("pig") "human torpedo," crewed by two frogmen who attached the torpedo's warhead to an enemy ship's hull. Four men crewed the British X-craft midget submarine, which carried two explosive charges and was a more advanced craft. Unlike these successful vessels, the design of the German Biber ("beaver") submarine was improvised. The craft was largely ineffective, despite being able to carry two full-size torpedoes. The vessels and other equipment used by modern undersea forces are considerably more sophisticated. For example, frogmen often use special underwater breathing apparatus that does not release air bubbles which would otherwise reveal their position.

Lifting eye

Bow

Towing eye

BRITISH X-CRAFT MIDGET SUBMARINE, WORLD WAR II (1939-1945)

Gearing for port side-cargo release mechanism

Battery compartment

Main hull frame

Main rotor ammeter

Gearing for starboard side-cargo release mechanism

Splashproof lamp

Air-pressure gauge

Hoist for external projector compass binnacle

Hull frame

Diving klaxon button

Diving klaxon

Remote controls for engine and motor

Log speed indicator

Trim and compensating pumps

Hydroplane wheel

Electrical switchboard

Battery charging regulator

Main electrical switchboard

Rudder shaft

Periscope

Hydroplane shaft

Secondary steering wheel

Distilled water tank

Main steering wheel

Freshwater tank

Flood valve for wet-and-dry chamber

Helmsman's seat

Wooden deckboard

Cradle for oxygen bottle

Log tank

Wet-and-dry exit and re-entry chamber

Kingston valve for main ballast tank

First lieutenant's seat frame

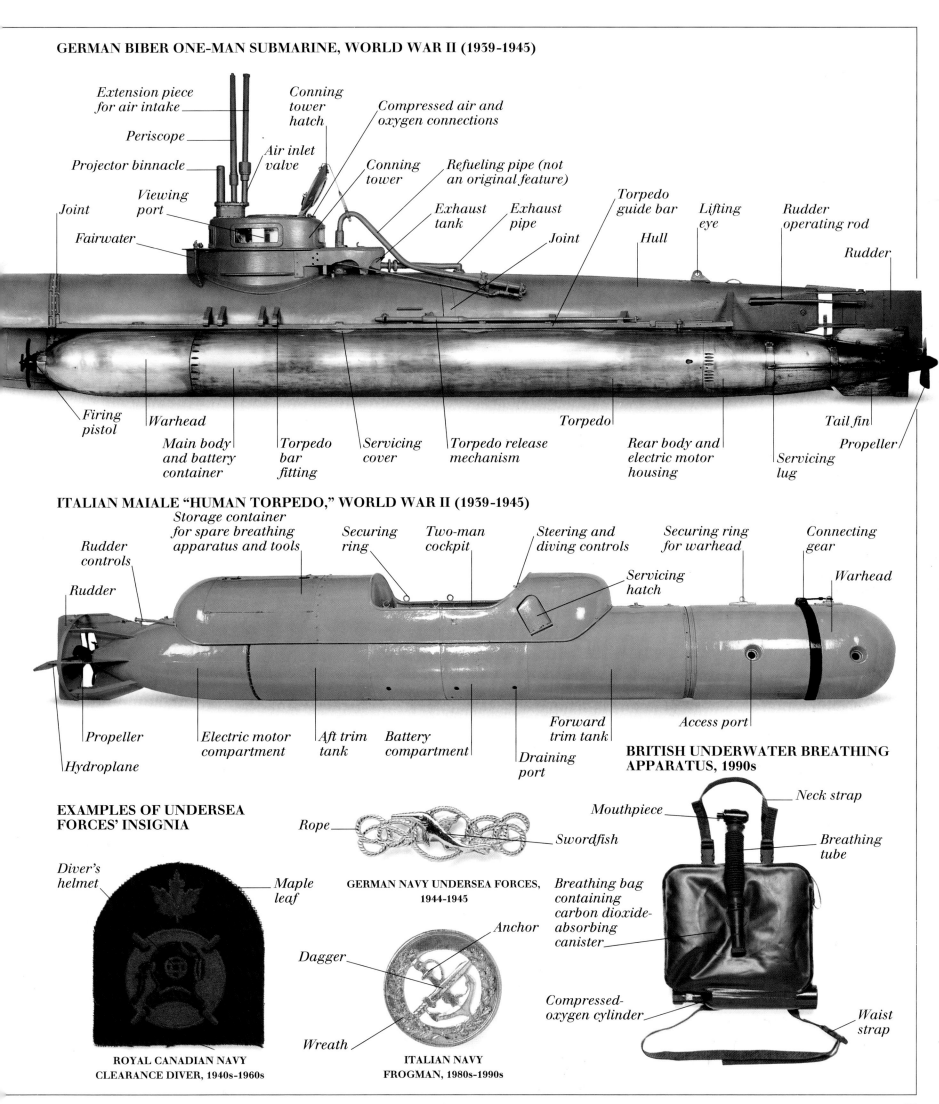

GERMAN BIBER ONE-MAN SUBMARINE, WORLD WAR II (1939-1945)

Extension piece for air intake
Periscope
Projector binnacle
Joint
Fairwater
Viewing port
Conning tower hatch
Air inlet valve
Conning tower
Compressed air and oxygen connections
Refueling pipe (not an original feature)
Exhaust tank
Exhaust pipe
Joint
Torpedo guide bar
Hull
Lifting eye
Rudder operating rod
Rudder

Firing pistol
Warhead
Main body and battery container
Torpedo bar fitting
Servicing cover
Torpedo release mechanism
Torpedo
Rear body and electric motor housing
Servicing lug
Tail fin
Propeller

ITALIAN MAIALE "HUMAN TORPEDO," WORLD WAR II (1939-1945)

Rudder controls
Rudder
Storage container for spare breathing apparatus and tools
Securing ring
Two-man cockpit
Steering and diving controls
Securing ring for warhead
Connecting gear
Servicing hatch
Warhead

Propeller
Hydroplane
Electric motor compartment
Aft trim tank
Battery compartment
Draining port
Forward trim tank
Access port

BRITISH UNDERWATER BREATHING APPARATUS, 1990s

Mouthpiece
Neck strap
Breathing tube
Breathing bag containing carbon dioxide-absorbing canister
Compressed-oxygen cylinder
Waist strap

EXAMPLES OF UNDERSEA FORCES' INSIGNIA

Rope
Swordfish

GERMAN NAVY UNDERSEA FORCES, 1944-1945

Diver's helmet
Maple leaf

ROYAL CANADIAN NAVY CLEARANCE DIVER, 1940s-1960s

Dagger
Anchor
Wreath

ITALIAN NAVY FROGMAN, 1980s-1990s

Parachutists 1

THE PRINCIPAL FUNCTION OF PARACHUTISTS is to land behind enemy lines to capture strategically important positions. Parachutists are equipped with two parachutes: a main one and a reserve, in case the main parachute fails to open. They are armed with lightweight and compact weapons, such as the U.S. M1A1 carbine, which has a folding skeleton stock. The shortage of supplies and vehicles at the landing area is a major problem for parachutists invading enemy territory. However, this problem can usually be overcome by parachuting equipment with the troops. For example, during World War II, containers holding weapons, ammunition, radios, and even folding motorcycles were parachuted down. Sometimes, larger vehicles were dropped by parachutes, such as the U.S. jeep, which needed four parachutes to land undamaged.

FRENCH PARACHUTISTS' CLOTHING, 1970s-1990s

Helmet with cover
Chin strap
Elastic strap
Shoulder strap
Parachutists' badge
Webbing suspenders strap
Belt
Ammunition pouch
Combat knife
Combat jacket
Pocket
Trousers
Reinforced ankle-support strap
Boot

SOVIET PARACHUTISTS' RPG 7D ROCKET-PROPELLED GRENADE LAUNCHER AND PG-7 ROCKET-PROPELLED GRENADE, 1960s-1990s

Headrest
Rubber eyepiece
On/off switch
Mounting bracket
Locking catch
Lens cap
Telescopic sight
Protective wings for emergency sight
Grenade-launcher tube
Protective wings for emergency sight
Guard
Disassembly catch
Trigger
Trigger guard
Screw fitting for guard
Pistol grip
Rear grip
Mounting bracket for telescopic sight
Rocket exhaust vent
Nose fuse
Warhead
Rocket exhaust vent
Collapsible stabilizing fin

BRITISH PARACHUTISTS' KNIFE, WORLD WAR II (1939-1945)

Spike
Lanyard loop
Grip
Blade lock and release catch
Manufacturer's mark
Blade

U.S. PARACHUTISTS' .30-CAL. M1A1 CARBINE, 1940s-1950s

Front sight
Hand guard
Bottle of oil and applicator
Rear sight
Trigger
Pistol grip
Trigger guard
Rear sling fitting
Barrel
Stock
Butt plate
Folding skeleton stock
10-round magazine

FRENCH FOREIGN LEGION INSIGNIA, 1970s

Bursting grenade

FRENCH FOREIGN LEGION ARM BADGE

Release handle

FRENCH FOREIGN LEGION CHEST BADGE, 2ND PARACHUTE REGIMENT

Static line

Harness

Main parachute

Reserve parachute

Rifle carrier

Lightweight pack

PARACHUTE EQUIPMENT ARRANGED FOR JUMP

FRENCH PARACHUTISTS' EQUIPMENT, 1970s

Spring fastener for static line

Buckle

Shoulder harness

Main parachute

Pocket for static line fastener

Reserve parachute

Securing lock for bar

Bar

Bottom strap

Pack strap

Lightweight pack

Pocket

Strap

Static line

Release button

Rifle carrier

Buckle for attaching reserve parachute

Pocket containing release rope

Release rope

Spring clip for release rope

Strap for rifle carrier

Eyelet for water bottle carrier

EXAMPLES OF PARACHUTISTS' INSIGNIA

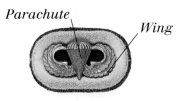

Parachute

Wing

U.S. PARACHUTIST, 1940s-1990s

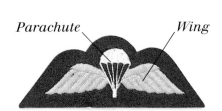

Parachute

Wing

BRITISH ARMY PARACHUTIST, 1940-1990s

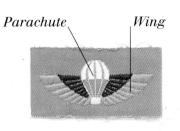

Parachute

Wing

AUSTRALIAN SPECIAL AIR SERVICE PARACHUTIST, 1960s-1990s

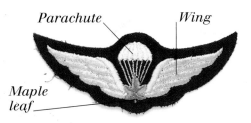

Parachute

Wing

Maple leaf

CANADIAN ARMY PARACHUTIST, 1940s-1960s

Parachutists 2

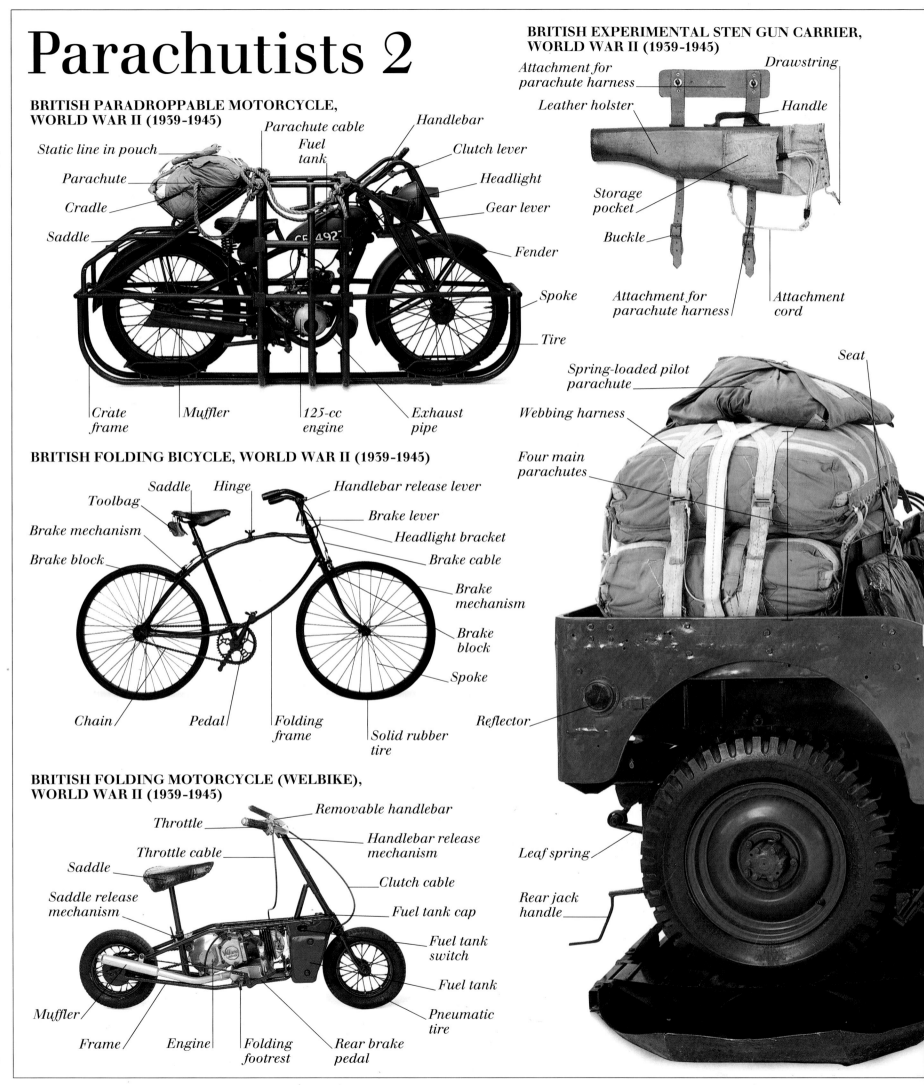

BRITISH PARADROPPABLE MOTORCYCLE, WORLD WAR II (1939-1945)

Parachute cable
Handlebar
Fuel tank
Clutch lever
Static line in pouch
Headlight
Parachute
Gear lever
Cradle
Saddle
Fender
Spoke
Tire
Crate frame
Muffler
125-cc engine
Exhaust pipe

BRITISH EXPERIMENTAL STEN GUN CARRIER, WORLD WAR II (1939-1945)

Attachment for parachute harness
Drawstring
Leather holster
Handle
Storage pocket
Buckle
Attachment for parachute harness
Attachment cord

BRITISH FOLDING BICYCLE, WORLD WAR II (1939-1945)

Saddle
Hinge
Handlebar release lever
Toolbag
Brake lever
Brake mechanism
Headlight bracket
Brake block
Brake cable
Brake mechanism
Brake block
Spoke
Chain
Pedal
Folding frame
Solid rubber tire

Seat
Spring-loaded pilot parachute
Webbing harness
Four main parachutes
Reflector
Leaf spring
Rear jack handle

BRITISH FOLDING MOTORCYCLE (WELBIKE), WORLD WAR II (1939-1945)

Removable handlebar
Throttle
Handlebar release mechanism
Throttle cable
Saddle
Clutch cable
Saddle release mechanism
Fuel tank cap
Fuel tank switch
Fuel tank
Muffler
Pneumatic tire
Frame
Engine
Folding footrest
Rear brake pedal

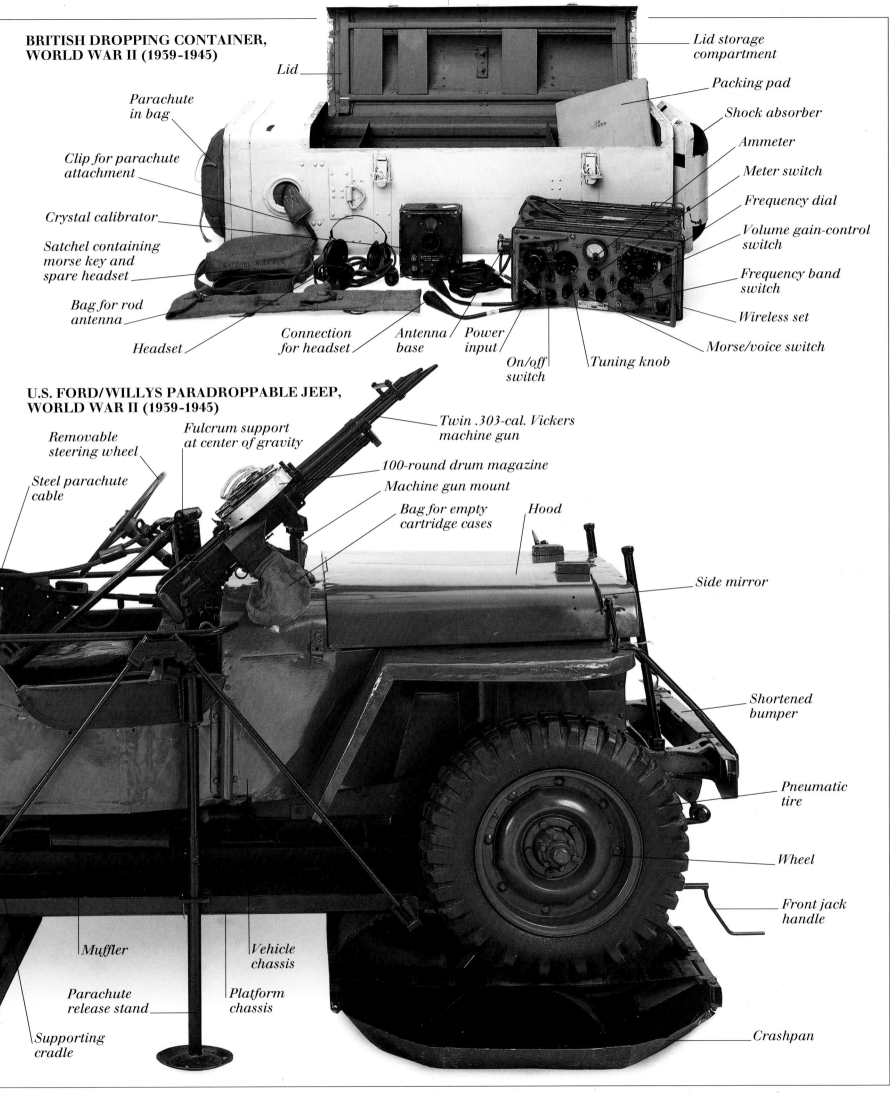

**BRITISH DROPPING CONTAINER,
WORLD WAR II (1939-1945)**

Lid storage
compartment

Lid

Packing pad

Shock absorber

Parachute
in bag

Ammeter

Meter switch

Clip for parachute
attachment

Frequency dial

Crystal calibrator

Volume gain-control
switch

Satchel containing
morse key and
spare headset

Frequency band
switch

Bag for rod
antenna

Wireless set

Morse/voice switch

Headset

Connection
for headset

Antenna
base

Power
input

On/off
switch

Tuning knob

**U.S. FORD/WILLYS PARADROPPABLE JEEP,
WORLD WAR II (1939-1945)**

Removable
steering wheel

Fulcrum support
at center of gravity

Twin .303-cal. Vickers
machine gun

Steel parachute
cable

100-round drum magazine

Machine gun mount

Bag for empty
cartridge cases

Hood

Side mirror

Shortened
bumper

Pneumatic
tire

Wheel

Front jack
handle

Muffler

Vehicle
chassis

Parachute
release stand

Platform
chassis

Supporting
cradle

Crashpan

Mountain forces

THE ARMED FORCES OF MANY NATIONS have troops specially trained in techniques of mountain warfare. These groups have to be skilled at climbing and at surviving in hostile mountain conditions, as well as being able to fight effectively in the difficult terrain. Mountain forces often use weapons that are specially adapted for the terrain. Howitzers are particularly suitable weapons for mountain warfare, because the barrel can be raised high enough to fire over peaks. As it is difficult to transport standard artillery in remote mountainous regions, specially modified guns are used. For example, the 3.7-inch mountain howitzer shown here has been adapted so that it can be broken down into eight parts, each of which is light enough to be carried by a mule.

EXAMPLES OF MOUNTAIN FORCES' INSIGNIA

Edelweiss

GERMAN ARMY, 24TH MOUNTAIN BRIGADE, 1950s–1990s

Edelweiss · Mountain

Regimental number

FRENCH ARMY, 159TH ALPINE REGIMENT, 1950s–1970s

Eagle
Mountain
Regimental number
Beacon
Italian Army crest

ITALIAN ARMY, 2ND ALPINE ARTILLERY REGIMENT, 1960s–1990s

BRITISH 3.7-IN MARK IV MOUNTAIN HOWITZER, WORLD WAR II (1939-1945)

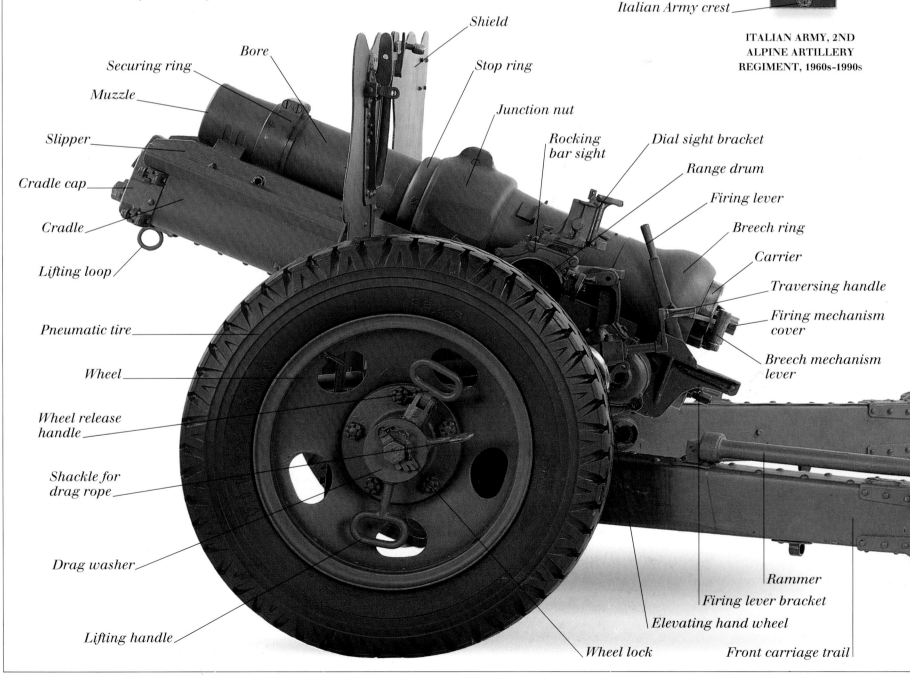

Shield
Bore
Securing ring
Muzzle
Slipper
Cradle cap
Cradle
Lifting loop
Stop ring
Junction nut
Rocking bar sight
Dial sight bracket
Range drum
Firing lever
Breech ring
Carrier
Traversing handle
Firing mechanism cover
Breech mechanism lever
Pneumatic tire
Wheel
Wheel release handle
Shackle for drag rope
Drag washer
Lifting handle
Rammer
Firing lever bracket
Elevating hand wheel
Wheel lock
Front carriage trail

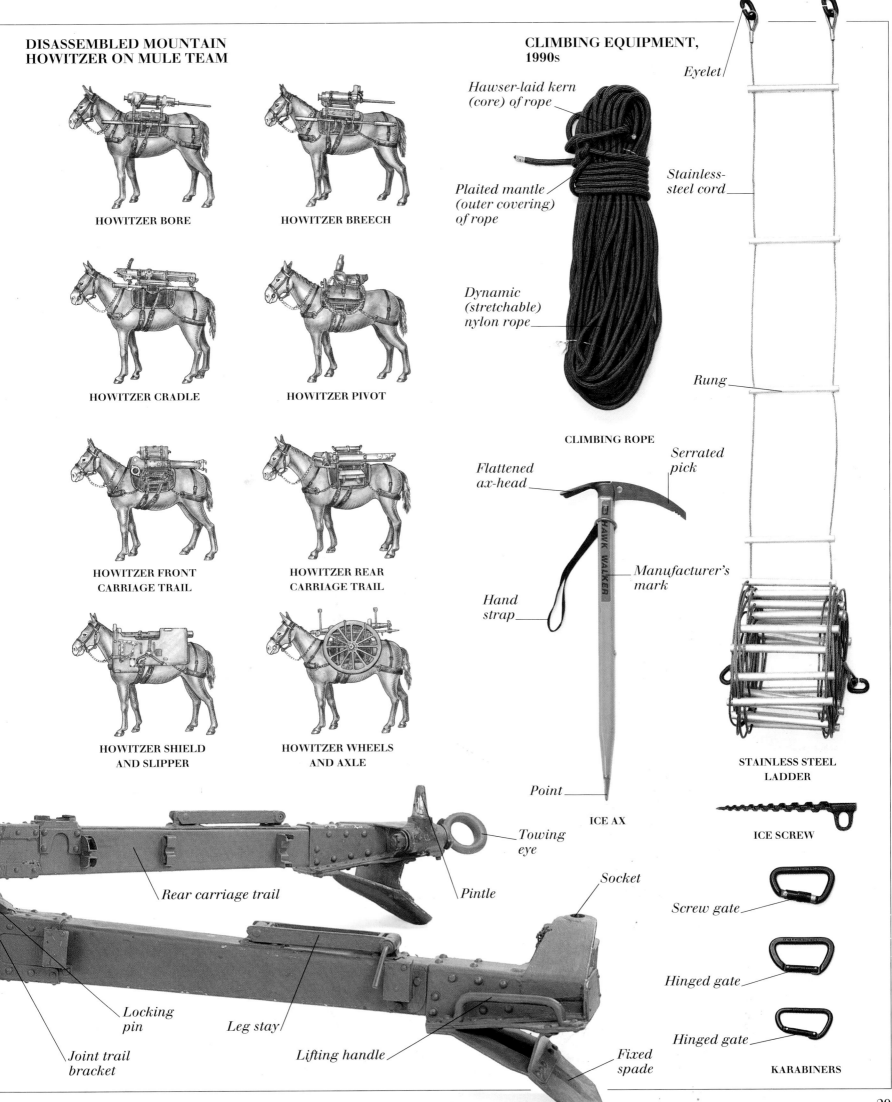

DISASSEMBLED MOUNTAIN HOWITZER ON MULE TEAM

HOWITZER BORE

HOWITZER BREECH

HOWITZER CRADLE

HOWITZER PIVOT

HOWITZER FRONT CARRIAGE TRAIL

HOWITZER REAR CARRIAGE TRAIL

HOWITZER SHIELD AND SLIPPER

HOWITZER WHEELS AND AXLE

CLIMBING EQUIPMENT, 1990s

Hawser-laid kern (core) of rope

Plaited mantle (outer covering) of rope

Dynamic (stretchable) nylon rope

CLIMBING ROPE

Eyelet

Stainless-steel cord

Rung

STAINLESS STEEL LADDER

Flattened ax-head

Serrated pick

Manufacturer's mark

Hand strap

Point

ICE AX

ICE SCREW

Towing eye

Rear carriage trail

Pintle

Socket

Screw gate

Hinged gate

Locking pin

Leg stay

Joint trail bracket

Lifting handle

Fixed spade

Hinged gate

KARABINERS

Arctic forces

THE ICY WILDERNESSES OF THE ARCTIC and Antarctic regions are among the most demanding environments in the world for military operations. In these regions, temperatures of -40°F (-40°C) are common, and the most important consideration is to ensure that troops keep warm enough to operate effectively. Consequently, the soldiers eat a high-energy diet and wear many layers of clothing, from an inner layer of thermal underwear to an outer snow-camouflage parka and trousers. They are also equipped with dark goggles to prevent snow blindness, face masks, insulated footwear, two or more pairs of gloves, and skis. Some weapons have been modified to make them suitable for use by Arctic forces. The Finnish Lahti anti-tank rifle, for example, is fitted with short skis for towing over snow and ice, and the Japanese Taisho pistol has an enlarged trigger guard so that it can be used when wearing thick gloves.

BRITAIN'S ROYAL MARINES' ARCTIC CLOTHING, 1990s

Snow goggles

Cotton combat shirt

Thermal vest

Quilted jacket

Elastic draft-proof cuff

Elastic draft-proof waist

Thermal underwear

Elastic draft-proof ankle band

Cotton combat trousers

BRITAIN'S ROYAL MARINES' ARCTIC FOOTWEAR, 1990s

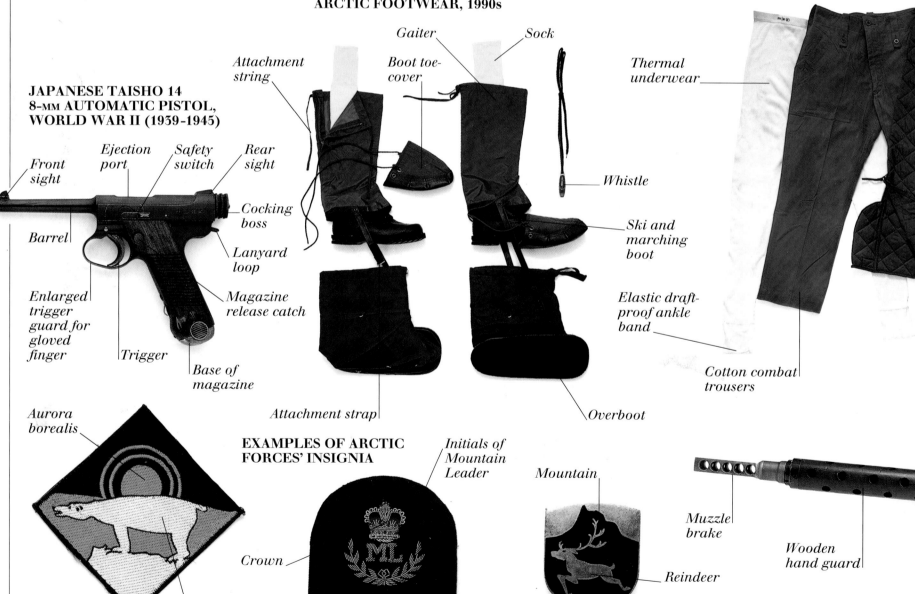

Gaiter

Sock

Boot toe-cover

Attachment string

JAPANESE TAISHO 14 8-MM AUTOMATIC PISTOL, WORLD WAR II (1939-1945)

Ejection port

Safety switch

Rear sight

Front sight

Cocking boss

Barrel

Lanyard loop

Enlarged trigger guard for gloved finger

Magazine release catch

Trigger

Base of magazine

Whistle

Ski and marching boot

Attachment strap

Overboot

Aurora borealis

EXAMPLES OF ARCTIC FORCES' INSIGNIA

Initials of Mountain Leader

Mountain

Muzzle brake

Crown

Wooden hand guard

Polar bear

Wreath

Reindeer

NORWEGIAN ARCTIC UNIT, 15TH ROYAL REGIMENT, 1950s-1990s

BRITAIN'S ROYAL MARINES MOUNTAIN AND ARCTIC CADRE, MOUNTAIN LEADER, 1981-1990s

ROYAL NETHERLANDS MARINE CORPS, ARCTIC UNIT, 1970s-1991

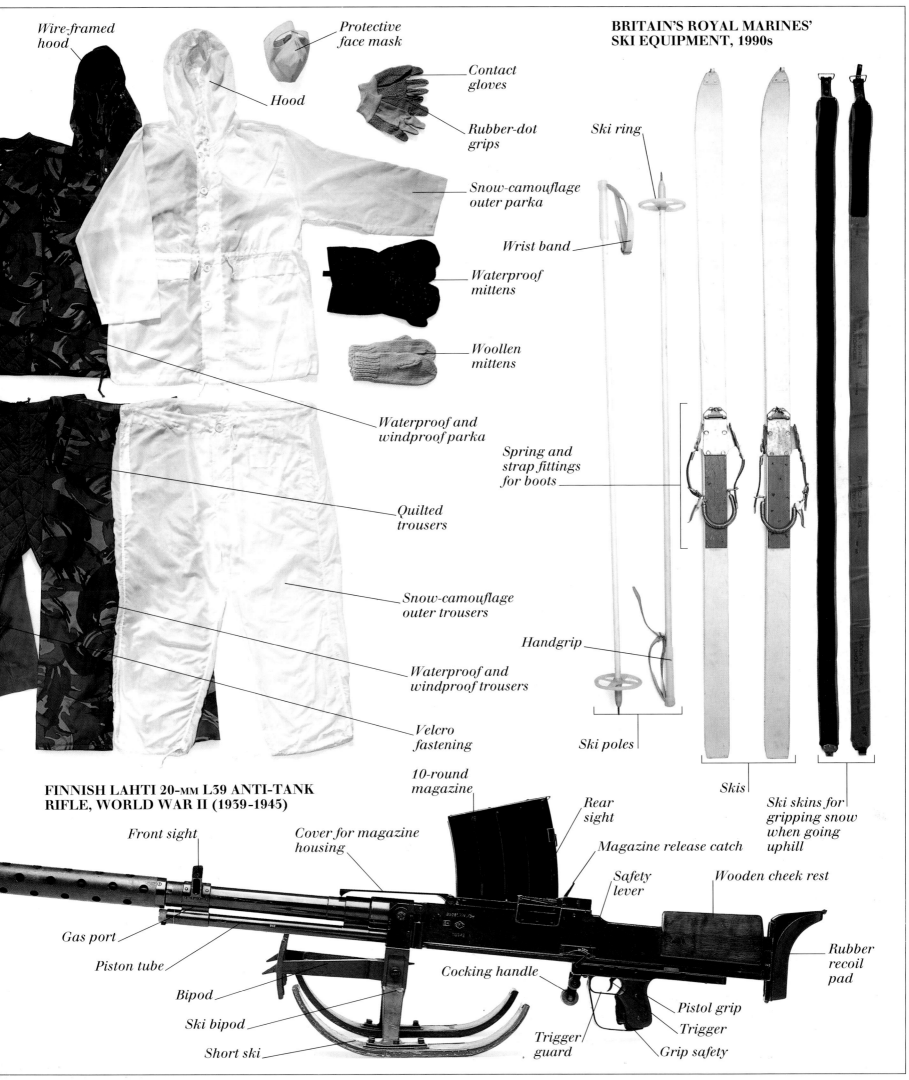

Wire-framed hood

Protective face mask

Hood

Contact gloves

Rubber-dot grips

Snow-camouflage outer parka

Wrist band

Waterproof mittens

Woollen mittens

Waterproof and windproof parka

Quilted trousers

Snow-camouflage outer trousers

Waterproof and windproof trousers

Velcro fastening

BRITAIN'S ROYAL MARINES' SKI EQUIPMENT, 1990s

Ski ring

Spring and strap fittings for boots

Handgrip

Ski poles

Skis

Ski skins for gripping snow when going uphill

FINNISH LAHTI 20-MM L39 ANTI-TANK RIFLE, WORLD WAR II (1939-1945)

10-round magazine

Rear sight

Cover for magazine housing

Magazine release catch

Front sight

Safety lever

Wooden cheek rest

Gas port

Piston tube

Cocking handle

Rubber recoil pad

Bipod

Ski bipod

Pistol grip

Short ski

Trigger guard

Trigger

Grip safety

Snipers

MANY SPECIAL FORCES HAVE SNIPERS who are trained to shoot at selected targets from a concealed position. As well as being a good marksman, a sniper must be an expert in concealment, in order to take the target unaware. Camouflage-patterned clothing, such as the modern gillie suit, helps disguise the sniper because it breaks up the outline of the body. Sniper rifles used to be standard rifles fitted with telescopic sights, such as the World War I Canadian Ross rifle. Later, however, rifles were developed specifically for snipers; examples include the Japanese Type 97 and the Soviet Dragunov rifles. Modern sniper rifles are extremely accurate and are made of new materials, including plastics. The latest weapons, such as the German Heckler and Koch sniper's rifle, can be adjusted to suit the individual sniper's requirements.

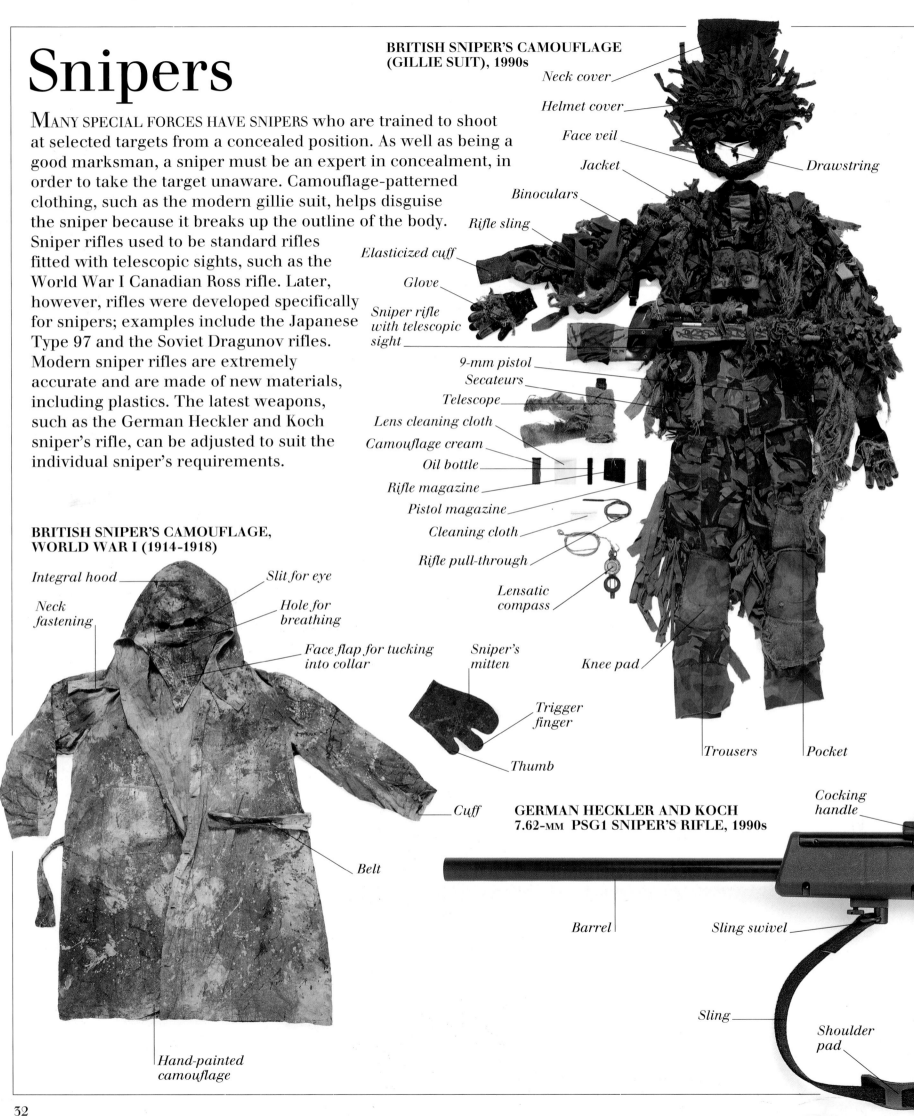

BRITISH SNIPER'S CAMOUFLAGE (GILLIE SUIT), 1990s

Neck cover

Helmet cover

Face veil

Jacket

Drawstring

Binoculars

Rifle sling

Elasticized cuff

Glove

Sniper rifle with telescopic sight

9-mm pistol

Secateurs

Telescope

Lens cleaning cloth

Camouflage cream

Oil bottle

Rifle magazine

Pistol magazine

Cleaning cloth

Rifle pull-through

Lensatic compass

Knee pad

Sniper's mitten

Trigger finger

Thumb

Trousers

Pocket

BRITISH SNIPER'S CAMOUFLAGE, WORLD WAR I (1914-1918)

Integral hood

Slit for eye

Neck fastening

Hole for breathing

Face flap for tucking into collar

Cuff

Belt

Hand-painted camouflage

GERMAN HECKLER AND KOCH 7.62-MM PSG1 SNIPER'S RIFLE, 1990s

Cocking handle

Barrel

Sling swivel

Sling

Shoulder pad

CANADIAN ROSS .303-CAL. MK III SNIPER'S RIFLE, WORLD WAR I (1914–1918)

Hooded front sight
Barrel
Barrel band
Hand guard
Range adjustment knob
Windage adjustment knob
Telescopic sight
Eyepiece
Straight-pull bolt
Bolt handle
Bayonet lug
Sling swivel
Sling swivel
Stock
Five-round magazine
Trigger guard
Trigger
Stock
Sling swivel

JAPANESE 6.5-mm TYPE 97 SNIPER'S RIFLE, c.1937

Front sight
Barrel
Barrel band
Hand guard
Sight mounting/dismounting catch
Battle sight
Rear sight
Telescopic sight
Bolt release catch
Bolt
Bolt handle
Eyepiece
Bolt cap
Cleaning rod
Folded monopod
Sling swivel
Stock
Finger groove
Magazine well
Trigger guard
Trigger
Bayonet lug
Sling
Stock
Stock plate

SOVIET DRAGUNOV 7.62-mm SNIPER'S RIFLE, c.1963

Hooded front sight
Barrel
Gas port
Piston tube
Sight mounting/dismounting catch
Elevation knob
Telescopic sight
Rear sight
Top cover
Eyepiece
Sling bar
Stock
Flash suppressor
Bayonet lug
Sling loop
Ventilation slot
Stock
Lens cover
10-round magazine
Magazine release
Trigger guard
Trigger
Pistol grip
Stock plate

Telescopic sight
Elevation adjustment control
Reticule lighting system
Battery housing cover
Lens cap
Eyepiece

Cocking handle slot
Disassembly bolt
Adjustable cheek rest
Plastic stock
Five-round magazine
Trigger guard
Safety switch
Adjustable stock plate
Trigger with adjustable shoe
Wooden pistol grip
Rubber hand rest
Plastic stock
Sling swivel

Special military vehicles

SPECIAL FORCES USUALLY OPERATE IN SMALL GROUPS and are often sent on missions to areas that are inaccessible to large contingents of conventional troops. Furthermore, the areas to which they are sent are often extremely inhospitable, with difficult terrain and harsh climates, such as deserts, mountains, and jungles. To transport people and equipment to such areas, and to operate effectively when they are there, special forces need vehicles that are reliable and adaptable. The U.S. High-Mobility, Multipurpose Wheeled Vehicle ("HUMVEE" or "HUMMER") has a four-wheel drive that enables it to be used in even the roughest conditions. It may also be adapted for other functions, such as that of an ambulance, a communications vehicle, or an armament carrier. The U.S. "Huey" helicopter was one of the first to be used specifically for military assaults. The Huey was used during the Vietnam War to land special forces in isolated jungle areas, as well as being used by conventional troops and as a helicopter gunship. For some covert missions, special forces may use lightweight boats, such as the Klepper Kayak, used by Britain's Special Boat Service. This kayak can be disassembled easily so that it can be carried by hand or dropped by parachute.

U.S. UH-1 ("HUEY") HELICOPTER, 1960s–1990s

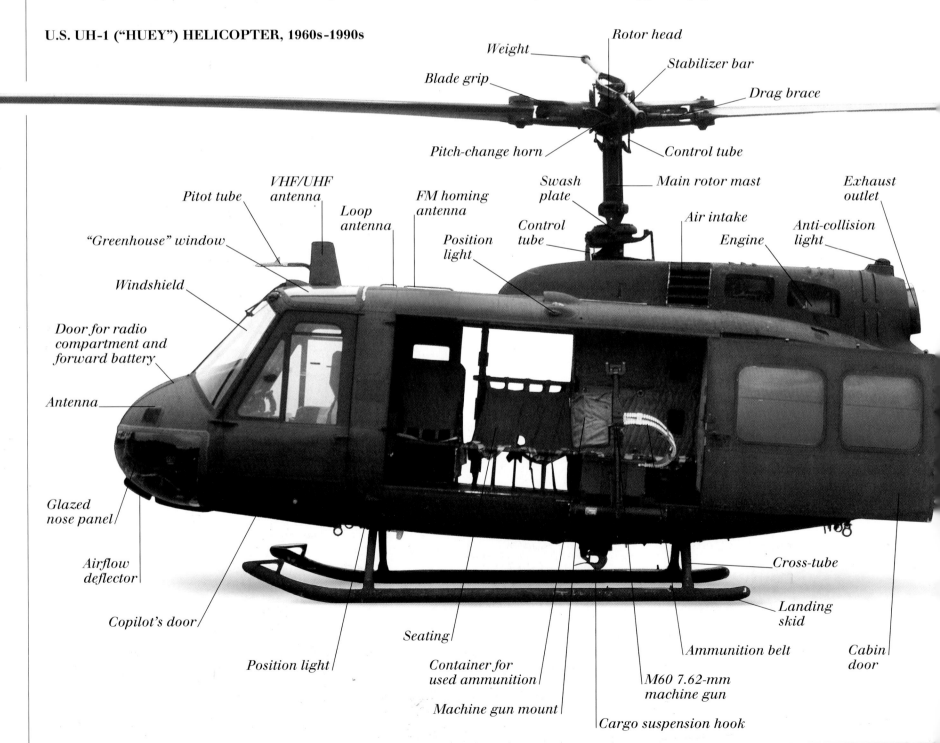

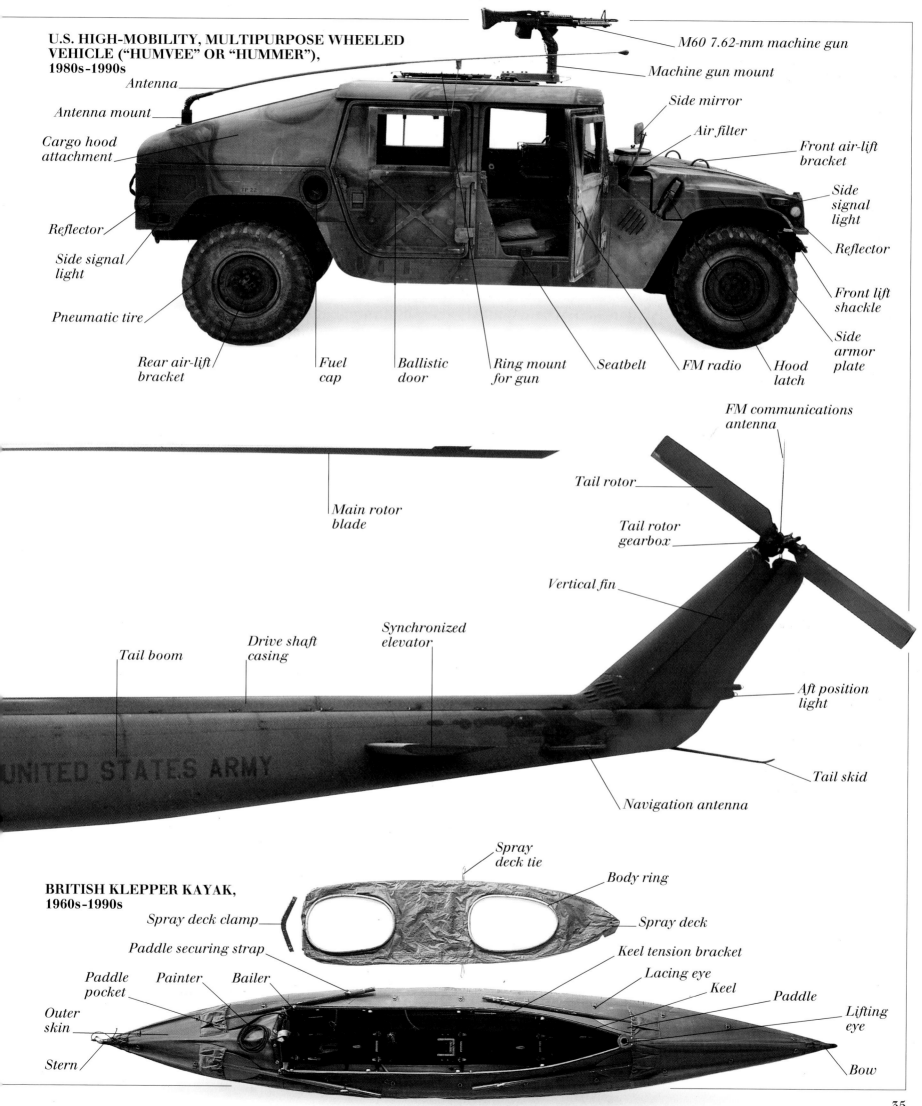

U.S. HIGH-MOBILITY, MULTIPURPOSE WHEELED VEHICLE ("HUMVEE" OR "HUMMER"), 1980s–1990s

M60 7.62-mm machine gun

Machine gun mount

Side mirror

Antenna

Air filter

Antenna mount

Front air-lift bracket

Cargo hood attachment

Side signal light

Reflector

Reflector

Side signal light

Front lift shackle

Pneumatic tire

Side armor plate

Rear air-lift bracket

Fuel cap

Ballistic door

Ring mount for gun

Seatbelt

FM radio

Hood latch

FM communications antenna

Main rotor blade

Tail rotor

Tail rotor gearbox

Vertical fin

Tail boom

Drive shaft casing

Synchronized elevator

Aft position light

UNITED STATES ARMY

Tail skid

Navigation antenna

BRITISH KLEPPER KAYAK, 1960s–1990s

Spray deck tie

Body ring

Spray deck clamp

Spray deck

Paddle securing strap

Keel tension bracket

Lacing eye

Paddle pocket

Painter

Bailer

Keel

Paddle

Outer skin

Lifting eye

Stern

Bow

Military surveillance

ARMED FORCES OFTEN USE clandestine surveillance – secret observation – to discover an enemy's movements and plans. There are two main groups of surveillance equipment: listening devices (commonly known as bugs), and visual surveillance equipment. Listening devices essentially consist of a microphone and transmitter. Such devices are small enough to be hidden inside many everyday objects, such as batteries or electric plugs. When in place, the listening device picks up sounds and transmits them to a listening post, which may be several miles away. Visual surveillance devices include relatively simple monoculars and cameras fitted with telephoto lenses, such as the Soviet Foto-Sniper camera, which may be used to obtain detailed photographs of distant objects. More sophisticated devices include night-vision goggles and special binocular telescopes fitted with electronic image-intensifiers that amplify ambient light so that it is possible to see in almost complete darkness.

YELLOW FILTER

ORANGE FILTER

ULTRAVIOLET FILTER

GREEN FILTER

YELLOW FILTER

U.S. ELECTRIC PLUG CONTAINING LISTENING DEVICE, 1960s

Electric plug casing

Listening device

Antenna

Pin

U.S. BATTERY INTERIOR CONTAINING LISTENING DEVICE, 1960s

Positive terminal

Inner battery casing

Antenna

Listening device

BRITISH MINIATURE MONOCULAR, WORLD WAR II (1939-1945)

Brass body

Eyepiece

SOVIET FOTO-SNIPER SURVEILLANCE CAMERA, 1960s–1970s

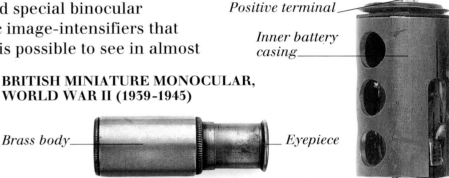

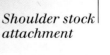

300-mm telephoto lens

Lens aperture ring

Kalimar SR-200 single lens reflex camera

Rubber eyecup

Spare 58-mm lens

Camera body locking mount

ФОТО СНАЙПЕР

Rubber lens hood

Shoulder strap fitting

Focusing ring

Securing device for holding lens to shoulder stock

Shutter-release trigger mechanism

Shutter-release trigger

Shoulder stock attachment

Pistol grip

Removable shoulder stock

Shoulder strap fitting

DUTCH NIGHT-VISION GOGGLES, 1990s

Adjustable head strap

Leather pad

Buckle

Head harness

Adjustable head strap

Leather face pad

Harness securing plate

Mask frame

Buckle

Viewer body

Battery cover

On/off switch

Rubber rim lens protector

Lens cap

Interocular adjustment bar

Lens

Hinge

Adjustable support bar

Adjustment lock

BRITISH SIMRAD DAY- AND NIGHT-VISION BINOCULAR TELESCOPE, 1990s

Daylight binocular telescope

Lens cover strap

Image intensifer casing

Diopter adjustment

Eyepiece

Lens cover

Focusing wheel

Shoulder stock

Battery position markings

On/off switch

Battery compartment

Battery lid

OFF ON   2 x 1,5V AA CELL

37

Espionage 1

THE MAIN PURPOSE OF ESPIONAGE is to gain secret information about an enemy. This clandestine work is carried out by agents of intelligence organizations, such as MI6 (the British Secret Service), the CIA (the U.S. Central Intelligence Agency), and the former Soviet Union's KGB (the Komitat Gosudarstvennoi Bezopasnosti). Such agents may be given false identities to enable them to move around freely in enemy territory without arousing suspicion. In some cases, they may be recruited from among the ranks of the enemy itself. Agents are trained in techniques of infiltrating high-security establishments and gathering information without being detected. To help them in these tasks, agents are often equipped with a variety of specially designed devices, such as concealed or disguised cameras and tape recorders, lockpicks, and portable photocopying machines.

U.S. LOCKPICK KNIFE, WORLD WAR II (1939-1945)

JAPANESE ECHO 8 CIGARETTE LIGHTER CAMERA, 1950s

Film slitter

Lid

Viewing port

Exposure setting lever

Aperture setting scale

Aperture setting knob

Lighter body

FRENCH ESPIONAGE CAMERA, WORLD WAR II (1939-1945)

Viewfinder openings

Lens

Lever for opening lens cover

Viewing port

Frame counter

Shutter release

Film advance knob

U.S. INTELLIGENCE SERVICES' PHOTO-SURVEILLANCE BRIEFCASE, 1960s

Fastening strap

Cable release

Winding knob

German Robot Star II 35-mm surveillance camera

Camera attachment bracket

Radionarf 38-mm lens

Lens opening

False lock

Slit for camera lens

Shutter release

Plastic mounting board

Buckle

Shutter release lever

SOVIET KGB CIGARETTE PACK CAMERA, 1970s

Metal facsimile pack of cigarettes

False cigarette

Internal mounting rail

Positioning clip

Lens

Shutter release

Kiev 30 camera

The House of John Player, Nottingham, England

The House of John Player, Nottingham, England

Film compartment

Aperture dial

Shutter speed dial

SOVIET F-21 TYPE II SURVEILLANCE CAMERA, 1970s-1980s

Pocket control unit

Thumb lever for setting aperture

Squeeze trigger for firing shutter

Remote shutter release cable

Frame counter

Winding knob

Shutter release

N°72749

Shutter speed dial

Lens

Locking collar

Synchronization lever

Attachment for waist belt

Camera cover

False button with opening for lens

Camera locking lever

SWISS ABC STEINECK WRIST CAMERA, 1950s

Wrist strap

Right-angle viewfinder

Lens

Film cassette indicator

Shutter release

Direct vision viewfinder

Setting for dim light

Aperture setting knob

Setting for bright light

Steineck AB-C

Manufacturer's mark

GERMAN MINOX MINIATURE CAMERA AND ACCESSORIES, 1960s

Focusing distance marker

Belt loop ring

MEASURING CHAIN

Attachment for camera

Handle

Negative holder

Eyepiece

NEGATIVE VIEWER

Development processing thermometer

Light-tight opening for adding developing liquid

Groove for film

Film holder

Thermometer case

Daylight developing tank

DAYLIGHT DEVELOPING KIT

Focusing dial

Frame counter

Shutter speed dial

Film speed dial

Shutter release

Lens

CAMERA

Meter cell

Viewfinder

Attachment to camera body

Reflector

FLASH ATTACHMENT

Camera attachment knob

Camera bracket

Opening for lens

Mirror

Right-angle viewing attachment

Opening for meter cell

Ball-and-socket joint

Legs of tripod (fit inside main leg)

Camera bracket

TRIPOD

Cable release

Telescopic leg

COPY STAND

Cable release

Rubber tip

Hollow main leg

Espionage 2

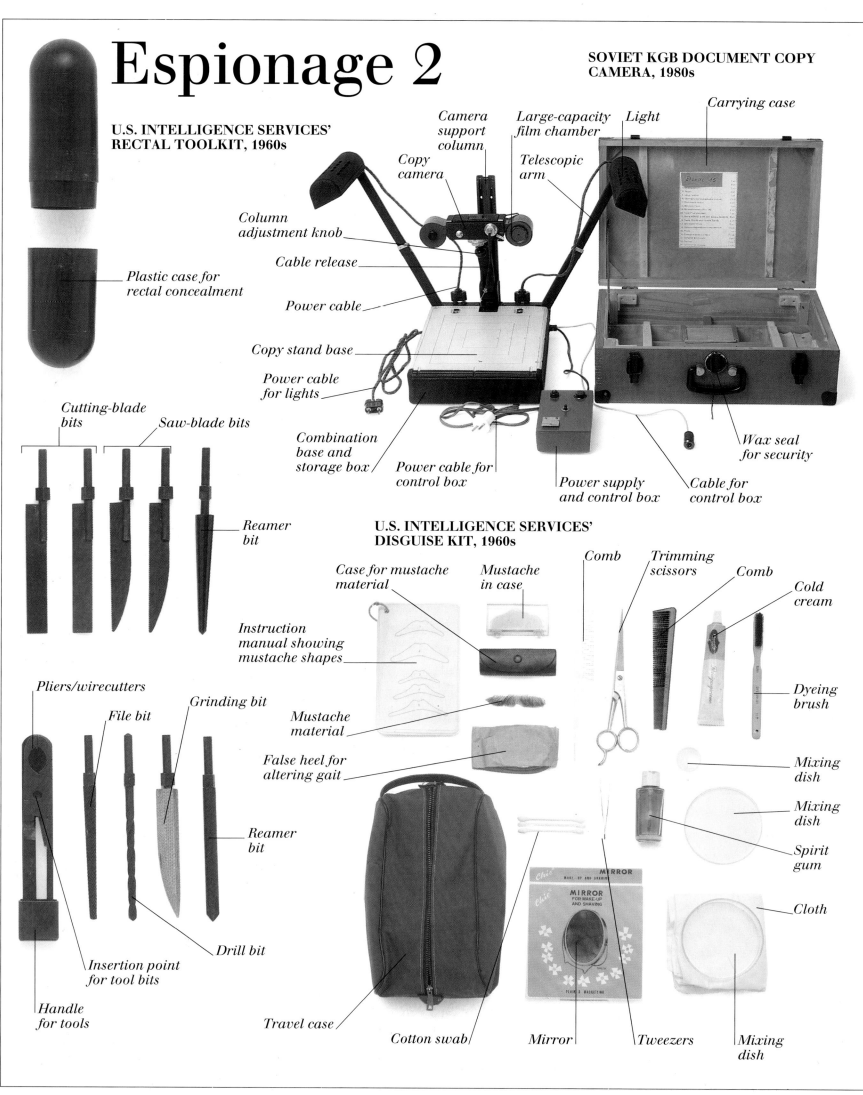

SOVIET KGB DOCUMENT COPY CAMERA, 1980s

U.S. INTELLIGENCE SERVICES' RECTAL TOOLKIT, 1960s

Plastic case for rectal concealment

Camera support column

Copy camera

Large-capacity film chamber

Light

Carrying case

Column adjustment knob

Telescopic arm

Cable release

Power cable

Copy stand base

Power cable for lights

Combination base and storage box

Power cable for control box

Power supply and control box

Cable for control box

Wax seal for security

Cutting-blade bits

Saw-blade bits

Reamer bit

U.S. INTELLIGENCE SERVICES' DISGUISE KIT, 1960s

Case for mustache material

Mustache in case

Comb

Trimming scissors

Comb

Cold cream

Instruction manual showing mustache shapes

Mustache material

False heel for altering gait

Dyeing brush

Pliers/wirecutters

File bit

Grinding bit

Reamer bit

Mixing dish

Mixing dish

Spirit gum

Drill bit

Insertion point for tool bits

Handle for tools

Travel case

Cotton swab

Mirror

Tweezers

Cloth

Mixing dish

U.S. INTELLIGENCE SERVICES' KEY-CASTING KIT, 1960s

Metal carrying case

Talcum powder

Extra clay

Packing material

Clay-filled aluminum mold for taking key impressions

Thimble holder

Thimble for melting alloy pellet

Low-melting-point alloy for casting keys

Candle (heat source)

Alloy pellet

U.S. INTELLIGENCE SERVICES' TAPE RECORDER AND TRANSCEIVER BRIEFCASE, 1960s–1970s

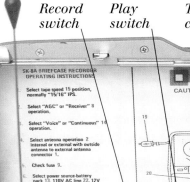

Record switch

Play switch

Tone control

Stop switch

Rewind switch

Operating instructions

Battery level indicator

Auxiliary socket

External antenna

Internal antenna

Reel-to-reel recorder

Speaker

Automatic gain control amplifier

Earphone socket

On/off switch

Receiver case

Internal/external antenna selection switch

Volume control

Adaptor for using car's power supply

Power cable

Volume control

Forward switch

Pilot lamp

Battery and accessories box

"Voice" or "Continuous" operation switch

Battery test light

Battery test button

Fuse holder

Automatic gain control/receiver selection switch

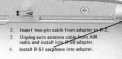

BELL & HOWELL

Earphone

Transmitter

Car antenna adapter

Car antenna and recorder adapter

Headphone

Clamp-on transformer

Microphone/ antenna

Sabotage

SABOTAGE IS THE COVERT destruction of important enemy equipment and installations, such as airfields, railways, and bridges. Acts of sabotage not only cause destruction but may also disrupt enemy movements, supply lines, and communications. Because of the need for secrecy, sabotage is usually carried out by individual agents or by small groups of special forces. Saboteurs often use plastic explosives, which may be molded into different shapes; other explosive devices used include grenades and demolition charges. These devices may be concealed or camouflaged, such as the magnetic "clam" demolition charge, which may be hidden on a vehicle, and the explosive disguised as coal, used to blow up steam engines. The explosives are often fitted with switches and time-delay fuses to enable saboteurs to escape unharmed.

BRITISH No.82 "GAMMON" GRENADE, WORLD WAR II (1939-1945)

BRITISH TIME-DELAY "PENCIL" FUSE, WORLD WAR II (1939-1945)

Fuse adapter/detonator holder

Colored safety strip indicating average time delay (black indicates 10 minutes)

Red (19 minutes)

White (1 hour 19 minutes)

Yellow (6 hours 30 minutes)

Blue (14 hours 30 minutes)

Body containing spring and striker

Copper crush tube containing ampule of corrosive liquid

Fixing screw

Metal case

U.S. KIT FOR MAKING "EXPLOSIVE COAL," WORLD WAR II (1939-1945)

Cloth

Paint

Turpentine

Case

Beeswax pellets

Polish

Shell for explosive disguised as a piece of coal

Pallet knife

Sticks

Hole for detonator

Penknife

Brushes

BRITISH No.36 M GRENADE ("MILLS BOMB"), WORLD WAR II (1939-1945)

Striker

Striker head

Filler plug

Body

Explosive chamber

Split ring

Safety pin

Spring

Striker chamber

Detonator

Lever

Fuse

Base plug

Percussion cap

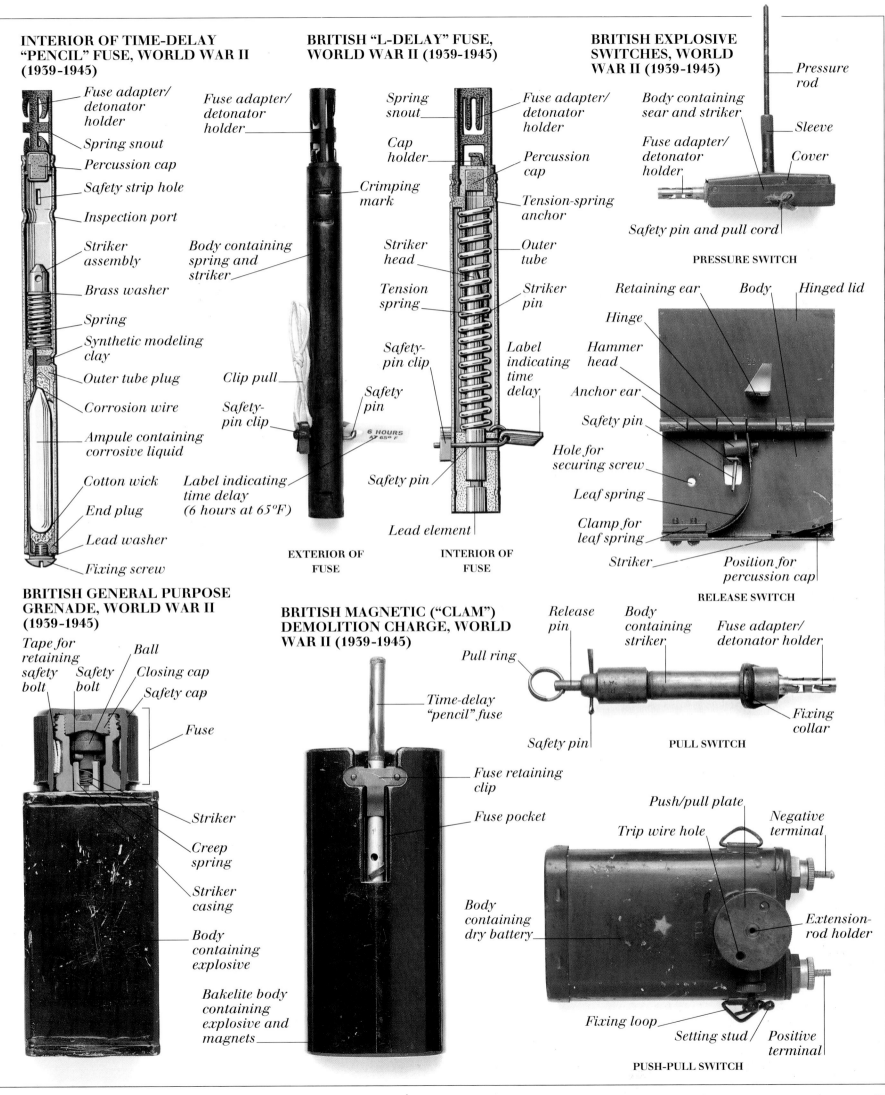

INTERIOR OF TIME-DELAY "PENCIL" FUSE, WORLD WAR II (1939-1945)

Fuse adapter/ detonator holder

Spring snout

Percussion cap

Safety strip hole

Inspection port

Striker assembly

Brass washer

Spring

Synthetic modeling clay

Outer tube plug

Corrosion wire

Ampule containing corrosive liquid

Cotton wick

End plug

Lead washer

Fixing screw

BRITISH "L-DELAY" FUSE, WORLD WAR II (1939-1945)

Fuse adapter/ detonator holder

Body containing spring and striker

Clip pull

Safety- pin clip

Label indicating time delay (6 hours at 65°F)

EXTERIOR OF FUSE

Spring snout

Cap holder

Striker head

Tension spring

Safety- pin clip

Safety pin

Safety pin

Fuse adapter/ detonator holder

Percussion cap

Tension-spring anchor

Outer tube

Striker pin

Label indicating time delay

Lead element

INTERIOR OF FUSE

BRITISH EXPLOSIVE SWITCHES, WORLD WAR II (1939-1945)

Pressure rod

Body containing sear and striker

Sleeve

Fuse adapter/ detonator holder

Cover

Safety pin and pull cord

PRESSURE SWITCH

Retaining ear

Body

Hinged lid

Hinge

Hammer head

Anchor ear

Safety pin

Hole for securing screw

Leaf spring

Clamp for leaf spring

Striker

Position for percussion cap

RELEASE SWITCH

BRITISH GENERAL PURPOSE GRENADE, WORLD WAR II (1939-1945)

Tape for retaining safety bolt

Ball

Safety bolt

Closing cap

Safety cap

Fuse

Striker

Creep spring

Striker casing

Body containing explosive

BRITISH MAGNETIC ("CLAM") DEMOLITION CHARGE, WORLD WAR II (1939-1945)

Time-delay "pencil" fuse

Fuse retaining clip

Fuse pocket

Body containing dry battery

Bakelite body containing explosive and magnets

Release pin

Body containing striker

Pull ring

Safety pin

Fuse adapter/ detonator holder

Fixing collar

PULL SWITCH

Push/pull plate

Trip wire hole

Negative terminal

Extension- rod holder

Fixing loop

Setting stud

Positive terminal

PUSH-PULL SWITCH

Counterrevolutionary units

BRITISH STUN GRENADE (EXPLODED), 1980s

THE GROWTH OF INTERNATIONAL terrorism has led to the formation of various elite counterrevolutionary forces, such as the Counter Revolutionary Unit of Britain's Special Air Service (SAS), Germany's Grenzschutzgruppe 9, part of the Bundesgrenschutz (German border guard), and the U.S. Delta Force. Soldiers in counterrevolutionary units undergo specialized training, not only in combat techniques, but also in methods of psychological warfare. Counterrevolutionary units usually operate in small teams of two or four men.

Typically, they wear protective body armor and are armed with special weapons, such as the light but accurate Heckler and Koch MP5 submachine gun, the Browning 9-mm automatic pistol, and magnesium-based stun grenades designed to shock terrorists without causing injury.

BRITISH SPECIAL AIR SERVICE BADGE, 1950-1990s

BRITISH SPECIAL AIR SERVICE'S HOLSTER, 1980s

Holster

Belt loop

Buckle

Magazine pouch

Retaining flap

Waist belt

Stud fastener

Browning 9-mm automatic pistol

Buckle

Webbing thigh strap

Attachment loop

GERMAN HECKLER AND KOCH 9-MM MP5A3 SUBMACHINE GUN, 1990s

Sling eye bolt

Front sight

Cocking handle

Bolt head carrier

Firing pin and spring

Hammer

Rotary rear sight

Pressure spring

Stock rail

Locking pin for hand guard

Locking piece

Guide rod

Recoil spring

Ejector

Rear sling fitting

Adjustable stock

Lug for securing blank firing device

Plastic hand guard

9-mm parabellum round

Locking pin for grip assembly

Follower and spring

30-round magazine

Magazine release catch

Trigger guard

Trigger

Sear

Locking pin for stock assembly

Single-shot position

Safety catch/ firing selector

Fully automatic position

Plastic pistol grip

BUNDESGRENZSCHUTZ

GERMAN BORDER GUARD (BUNDESGRENZSCHUTZ) BADGES, 1972-1990s

BRITISH SPECIAL AIR SERVICE'S PERSONAL EQUIPMENT, 1980s

Eyepiece

Head strap

Filter canister

Gas mask

Knife sheath

Knife

Collar

Eyehole

Mouth hole

Hood

Equipment loop

Stud fastener

Black suede combat vest

Black cotton overall

Leather glove

Grenade loop

Adjustable lace fastener

Wrist fastener

Equipment pocket

Grenade pocket

Shoulder strap

Stud fastener

Leather glove

Body armor

Thigh pocket

Side panel

Waist belt loop

Stud fastener

Velcro attachment strip

Body armor panel

Buckle

Thigh strap

Magazine pouch

Reinforced toecap

Leather boot

Leather boot

Leather boot

Military communications 1

GOOD COMMUNICATIONS ARE VITAL for the success of any military operation, and a wide variety of methods have been employed. One of the more unusual methods, used during World War II, involved parachuting homing pigeons to agents and special forces on the ground, so that the birds could carry messages when they flew home. Efficient communications are particularly important for special forces and secret agents because they often work alone or in small groups, and in remote and dangerous areas. They commonly use equipment that is portable and easy to conceal, such as walkie-talkies, "biscuit-tin" radio receivers, and suitcase radios. Keeping communications secure is also important. One way of achieving this is to use special methods of radio transmission. For example, the high-speed burst transmitter sends radio messages in short spurts, so that they cannot be intercepted easily. Another method of keeping communications secret is to send messages in code (see pp. 50-51).

Strap to fasten ring to pigeon's leg

Clip to fasten ring to pigeon's leg

Message carrier cap

Message carrier

Split stem on which message is rolled

BRITISH PIGEON PARACHUTE, WORLD WAR II (1939-1945)

Dropping handle

Securing harness for pigeon container

Parachute lines

Clip for harness

Parachute

Container for pigeon

Air hole

BRITISH MCR 1 RECEIVER ("BISCUIT-TIN" RECEIVER), WORLD WAR II (1939-1945)

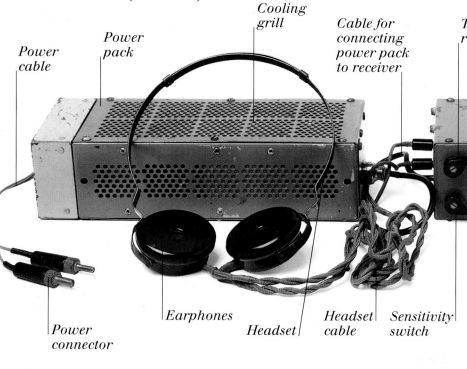

Power cable

Power pack

Cooling grill

Cable for connecting power pack to receiver

Tuner for telegraph reception

Antenna adjustment switch

Receiver

Frequency indicator

Frequency dial

Pin for attaching coil unit

Coil unit

REACTION

SENSITIVITY

AE TRIMMER

Coil unit

Power connector

Earphones

Headset

Headset cable

Sensitivity switch

Hole for receiver pin

Coil unit

Frequency-conversion scale

BRITISH TYPE A MK III SUITCASE RADIO, WORLD WAR II (1939-1945)

Corner strengthener

Cooling grill

Milliammeter for tuning transmitter

Padding to protect crystal

Negative ground terminal

Vibrator socket

On/off switch

Quartz crystal plate

Transmission/reception switch

Voltage selector

Cooling grill

AC/DC switch

Antenna connector

Tuner for telegraph reception

Morse key plug

Spare parts box

Transmitter tuning knobs

Power cable

Morse key cable

Power connector

Neon frequency-control tube

SPARES

Suitcase

Morse key cable

Frequency dial

Headset plug

Volume control

Cooling grill

Frequency wavelength switch

Morse key

Headset

Headset cable

Screwdriver

Power connectors

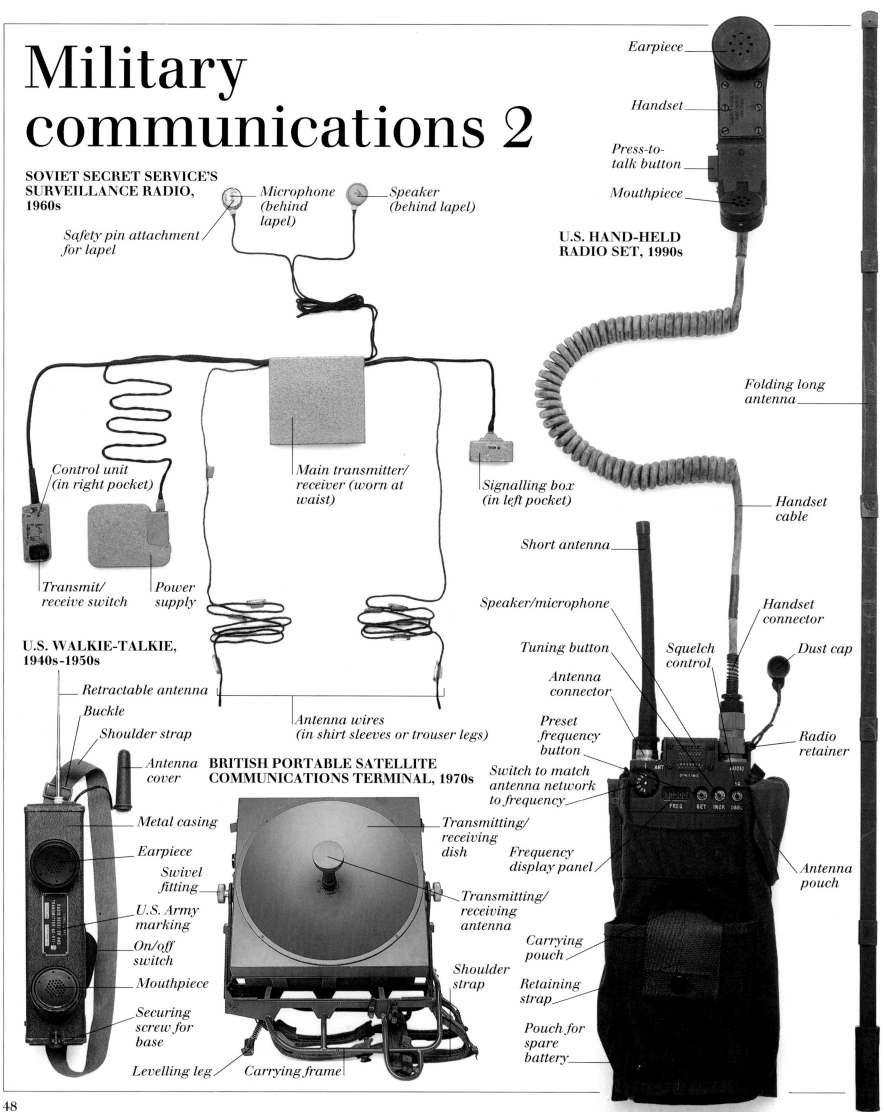

Military communications 2

SOVIET SECRET SERVICE'S SURVEILLANCE RADIO, 1960s

Microphone (behind lapel)

Speaker (behind lapel)

Safety pin attachment for lapel

Control unit (in right pocket)

Main transmitter/receiver (worn at waist)

Signalling box (in left pocket)

Transmit/receive switch

Power supply

U.S. WALKIE-TALKIE, 1940s-1950s

Retractable antenna

Antenna wires (in shirt sleeves or trouser legs)

Buckle

Shoulder strap

Antenna cover

BRITISH PORTABLE SATELLITE COMMUNICATIONS TERMINAL, 1970s

Metal casing

Earpiece

Swivel fitting

U.S. Army marking

On/off switch

Mouthpiece

Securing screw for base

Levelling leg

Carrying frame

Transmitting/receiving dish

Transmitting/receiving antenna

Shoulder strap

U.S. HAND-HELD RADIO SET, 1990s

Earpiece

Handset

Press-to-talk button

Mouthpiece

Folding long antenna

Handset cable

Short antenna

Speaker/microphone

Tuning button

Squelch control

Handset connector

Dust cap

Antenna connector

Preset frequency button

Switch to match antenna network to frequency

Radio retainer

Frequency display panel

Antenna pouch

Carrying pouch

Retaining strap

Pouch for spare battery

BRITISH A16 HF TRANSCEIVER USED BY SPECIAL AIR SERVICE, 1960s-1980s

Meter

Antenna connector

Morse alphabet

Waterproof socket cover

Cassette lid

Winding handle

Cassette tape with morse message

Frequency selector switches

High-speed "burst" transmitter

Format switch

Coded dial

Locating pin for cassette

Transfer head

Morse coder for cassette tape

Battery cable

Cassette lid

Cassette

Morse key

Dial for coding message in morse

Dash key

Space key

Dot key

Volume control

Squelch control

Transfer handle

Morse keys

Transmit switch

Transmitter/ receiver cable

Reel

Earphone cable

Flexible antenna

Pulley for antenna

Head strap

Earphone

Encoding and decoding

*Encoding and
decoding key*

*Pad used by base
for encoding and
decoding*

THE SENDING OF MESSAGES in code developed out
of the need to keep military communications
secret. Although codes (also known as ciphers)
have been used for centuries, they became
essential once radio was used to send messages,
because the enemy could easily intercept radio
transmissions. As the importance of encoding
increased, so too did the work of breaking codes.

**BRITISH CIPHER
WHEEL c.1880**

During World War II, one-time pads (so called because each sheet was used
once only) provided an almost totally safe method of encoding and decoding,
but using them took a long time. Faster methods of encoding had to be developed for use
by troops in action, so machines such as the compact U.S. M-209-B cipher machine were
designed. The German electromechanical Enigma machine had an extremely sophisticated
enciphering process that produced complex codes. The Enigma system was thought to be
completely secure, but it was eventually cracked by the Allies.

*Extra
key*

*Pad used by
agent for
encoding and
decoding*

**U.S. M-209-B CIPHER MACHINE,
WORLD WAR II (1939-1945)**

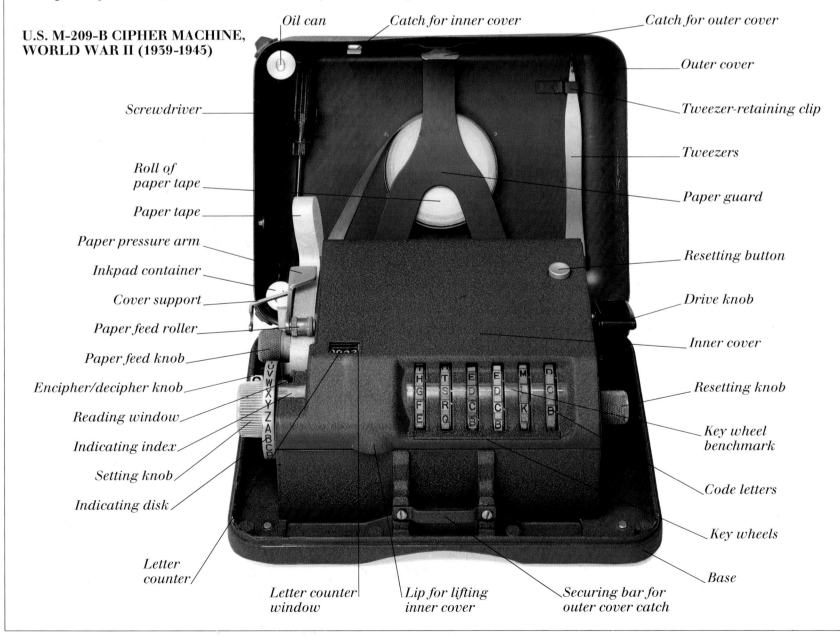

Oil can
Catch for inner cover
Catch for outer cover
Outer cover
Screwdriver
Tweezer-retaining clip
Tweezers
*Roll of
paper tape*
Paper tape
Paper guard
Paper pressure arm
Inkpad container
Resetting button
Cover support
Drive knob
Paper feed roller
Inner cover
Paper feed knob
Encipher/decipher knob
Resetting knob
Reading window
Indicating index
*Key wheel
benchmark*
Setting knob
Indicating disk
Code letters
Key wheels
*Letter
counter*
Base
*Letter counter
window*
*Lip for lifting
inner cover*
*Securing bar for
outer cover catch*

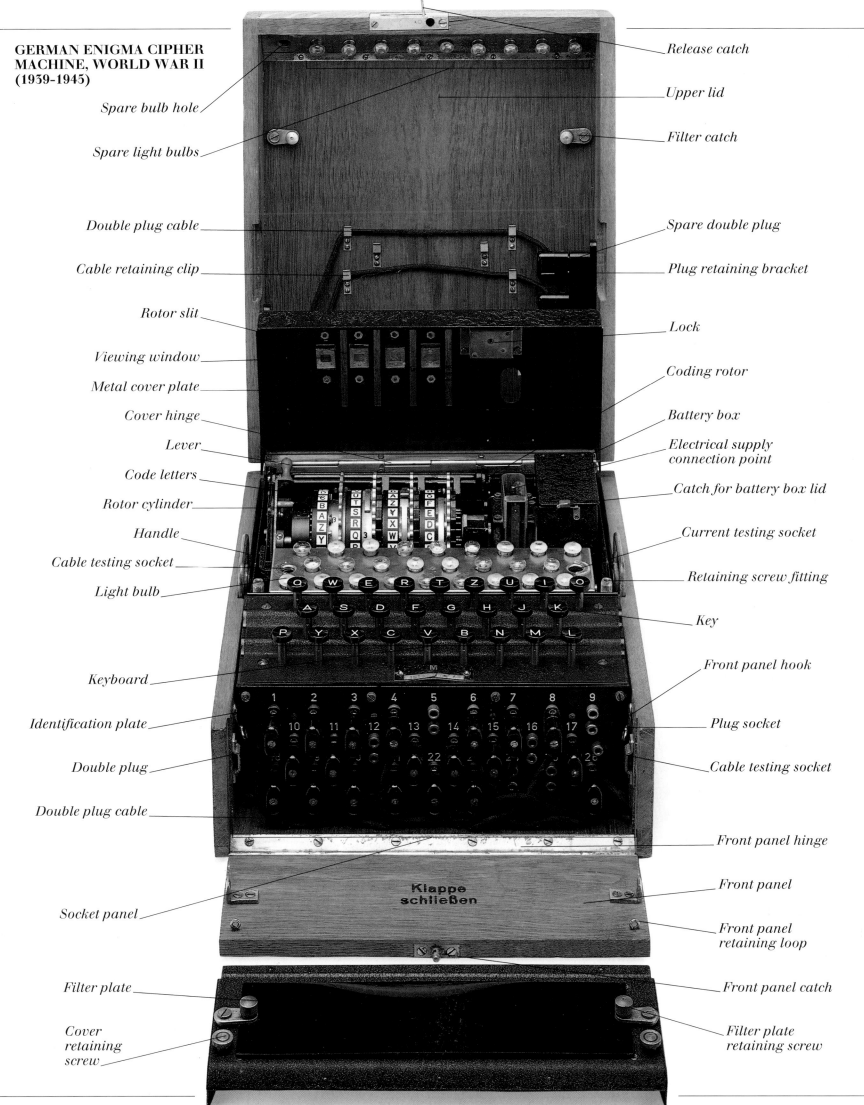

GERMAN ENIGMA CIPHER MACHINE, WORLD WAR II (1939-1945)

Release catch

Spare bulb hole

Upper lid

Spare light bulbs

Filter catch

Double plug cable

Spare double plug

Cable retaining clip

Plug retaining bracket

Rotor slit

Lock

Viewing window

Coding rotor

Metal cover plate

Battery box

Cover hinge

Electrical supply connection point

Lever

Code letters

Catch for battery box lid

Rotor cylinder

Current testing socket

Handle

Cable testing socket

Retaining screw fitting

Light bulb

Key

Keyboard

Front panel hook

Identification plate

Plug socket

Double plug

Cable testing socket

Double plug cable

Front panel hinge

Front panel

Socket panel

Front panel retaining loop

Klappe schließen

Filter plate

Front panel catch

Cover retaining screw

Filter plate retaining screw

Special forces weapons 1

SPECIAL FORCES HAVE TO CARRY OUT such a wide variety of missions that they have a great need for specialized weapons. For example, many of the clandestine operations undertaken by special forces require silent weapons, such as the special silenced version of the Sten submachine gun, which was used in World War II, or the modern version of a crossbow. In other dangerous situations – when fighting terrorists, for instance – special forces often require maximum firepower, and therefore many groups use pump-action shotguns, such as the Italian Franchi Special Purpose Automatic Shotgun, which is capable of firing four rounds per second. The M79 grenade launcher is used for longer-range action, because it can lob grenades and other explosive projectiles up to a distance of about 500 yards (450 m). Multipurpose weapons were popular with special forces involved in close-quarter fighting during World War II, when the knuckleduster knife and the Peskett close-combat weapon (comprising a garrotte, dagger, and bludgeon) were used.

Bomb head

Attachment for tail

Percussion fuse

Attachment for head

Propellant container

Hollow tail

Tail cover

Firing pin

Spigot

Firing wire

Safety pin

Clip for tail

Clamping screw

Mounting handle

Firing-wire guide

Clamping plate

Universal joint

Mounting screw

BRITISH TREE SPIGOT MORTAR, WORLD WAR II (1939-1945)

Hinge

Lens

Clamping screw

Calibrated adjustment arc

Spigot sleeve

Viewing aperture

LENSATIC SIGHT OF SPIGOT MORTAR

Shield cowl

Attachment clip

RAINSHIELD OF SPIGOT MORTAR

Suppressor (silencer)

U.S. BARRETT .50-CAL. M82A1 SPECIAL APPLICATIONS RIFLE, 1990s

Muzzle brake

Barrel

Emergency front sight

Sling fitting

Bipod lug

Hinge screw

Folding bipod

Stud for adjusting foot

Bipod foot

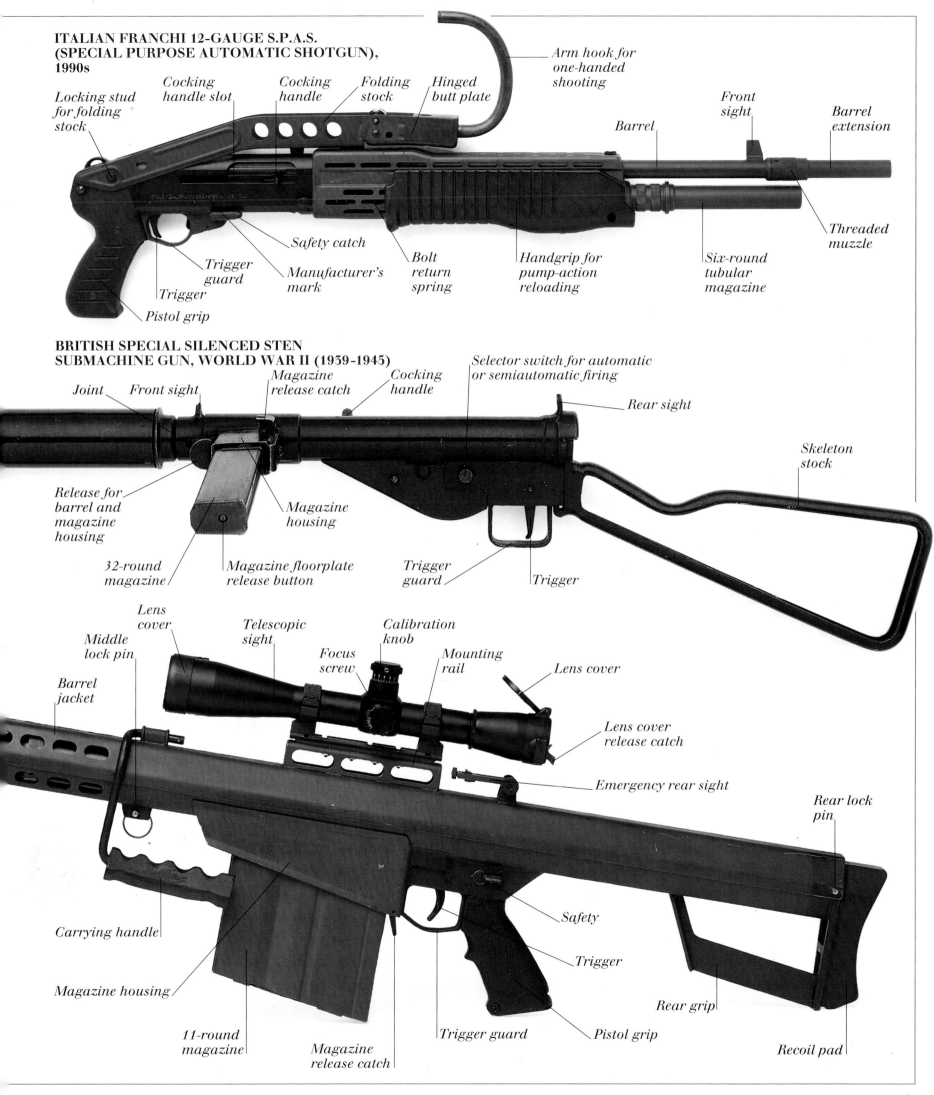

ITALIAN FRANCHI 12-GAUGE S.P.A.S. (SPECIAL PURPOSE AUTOMATIC SHOTGUN), 1990s

Locking stud for folding stock

Cocking handle slot

Cocking handle

Folding stock

Hinged butt plate

Arm hook for one-handed shooting

Front sight

Barrel

Barrel extension

Safety catch

Bolt return spring

Handgrip for pump-action reloading

Six-round tubular magazine

Threaded muzzle

Trigger guard

Manufacturer's mark

Trigger

Pistol grip

BRITISH SPECIAL SILENCED STEN SUBMACHINE GUN, WORLD WAR II (1939-1945)

Selector switch for automatic or semiautomatic firing

Joint

Front sight

Magazine release catch

Cocking handle

Rear sight

Skeleton stock

Release for barrel and magazine housing

Magazine housing

32-round magazine

Magazine floorplate release button

Trigger guard

Trigger

Lens cover

Telescopic sight

Calibration knob

Middle lock pin

Focus screw

Mounting rail

Lens cover

Barrel jacket

Lens cover release catch

Emergency rear sight

Rear lock pin

Carrying handle

Safety

Magazine housing

Trigger

11-round magazine

Magazine release catch

Trigger guard

Pistol grip

Rear grip

Recoil pad

53

Special forces weapons 2

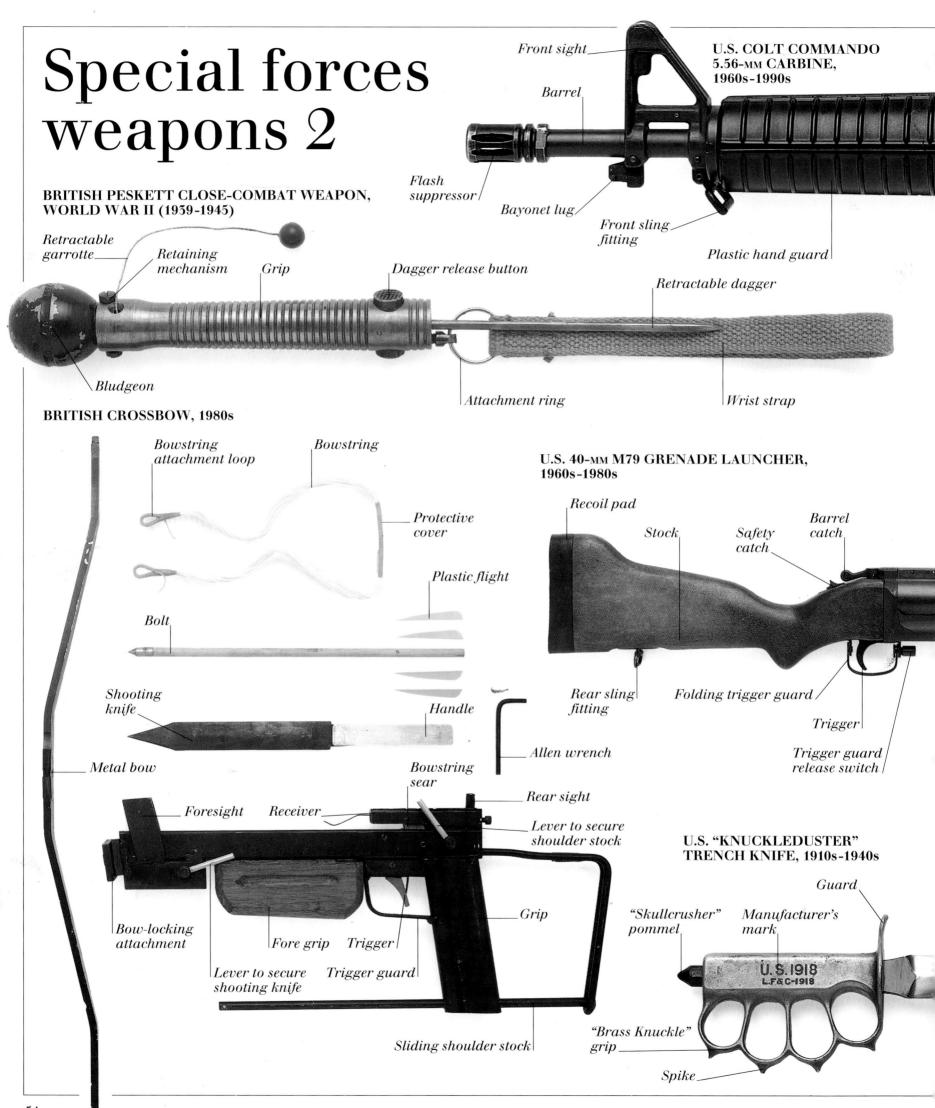

U.S. COLT COMMANDO 5.56-MM CARBINE, 1960s–1990s

Front sight

Barrel

Flash suppressor

Bayonet lug

Front sling fitting

Plastic hand guard

BRITISH PESKETT CLOSE-COMBAT WEAPON, WORLD WAR II (1939–1945)

Retractable garrotte

Retaining mechanism

Grip

Dagger release button

Retractable dagger

Bludgeon

Attachment ring

Wrist strap

BRITISH CROSSBOW, 1980s

Bowstring attachment loop

Bowstring

Protective cover

Plastic flight

Bolt

U.S. 40-MM M79 GRENADE LAUNCHER, 1960s–1980s

Recoil pad

Stock

Safety catch

Barrel catch

Shooting knife

Handle

Rear sling fitting

Folding trigger guard

Trigger

Trigger guard release switch

Metal bow

Allen wrench

Foresight

Receiver

Bowstring sear

Rear sight

Lever to secure shoulder stock

Bow-locking attachment

Fore grip

Trigger

Grip

U.S. "KNUCKLEDUSTER" TRENCH KNIFE, 1910s–1940s

Guard

"Skullcrusher" pommel

Manufacturer's mark

Lever to secure shooting knife

Trigger guard

U.S. 1918
L.F&C-1918

"Brass Knuckle" grip

Sliding shoulder stock

Spike

Carrying handle

Charging handle

Rear sling fitting

Bolt release catch

Extendible stock

Catch to extend stock

Safety catch/ firing selector

Slip ring

Plastic pistol grip

Trigger guard

Trigger

GERMAN HECKLER AND KOCH 9-мм P9S AUTOMATIC PISTOL, 1980s-1990s

30-round magazine

Front sight

Slide catch

Safety catch

Rear sight

Muzzle

Rear sight

Windage screw

Front sight

Slide

Barrel

Barrel clamp

Fore-end

Front of trigger guard for two-handed grip

Front sling fitting

Trigger

Trigger guard

Cocking lever

Pistol grip

AUSTRALIAN OWEN SUBMACHINE GUN, 1940s-1960s

33-round magazine

Magazine housing

Magazine release catch

Magazine floorplate

Magazine release catch

Selector switch

Front sight

Barrel

Disassembly plunger

Rear sight

Compensator

Ejection port

Stock

Front sling fitting

Trigger guard

Trigger

Pistol grip

Blade

Front grip

Rear sling fitting

Escape and survival 1

SPECIAL FORCES OPERATE in some of the most dangerous areas in the world, and so they have a relatively high chance of being captured by the enemy or stranded in hostile territory. Special forces are trained in survival techniques that give them a range of skills, including how to provide themselves with basic necessities, such as food, water, shelter, and fire, in even the most barren regions. Troops usually carry survival aids in pouches attached to their belts or web gear. If this type of kit is too bulky, a compact version of the survival kit, packed in a small container, can be carried. As well as being able to keep themselves alive, soldiers and aircrew must be able to attract help in an emergency, for instance, by lighting flares or by using a Search and Rescue Beacon (SARBE) to signal their location and speak to the rescuer. Agents and special forces operating in enemy territory may suddenly be forced to escape from the country, so they carry compasses and maps. For situations in which troops may have to identify themselves in foreign countries, they are issued with an emergency kit that includes "blood chits," which display the troops' national flag and show useful phrases in local languages.

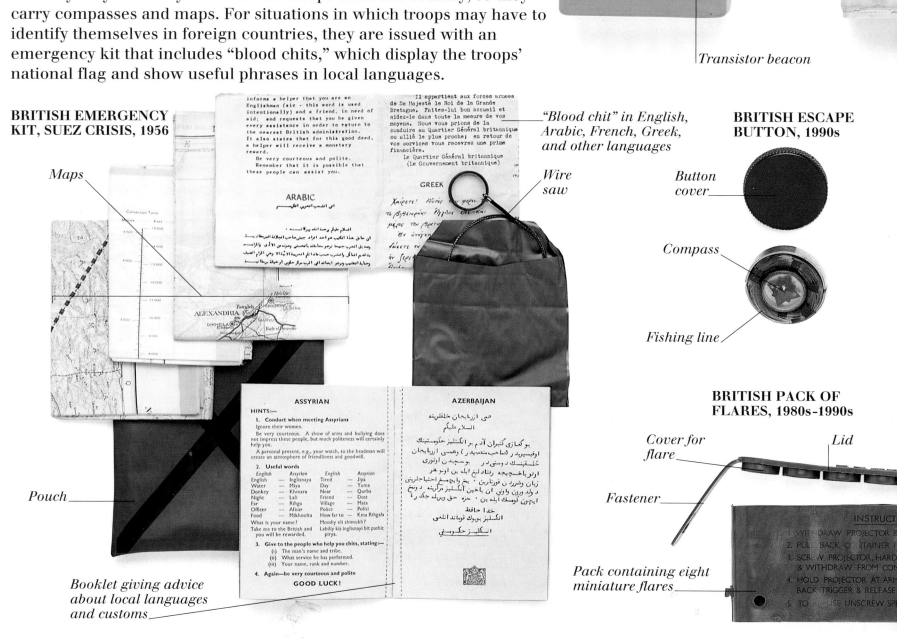

Connecting lead

BRITISH SEARCH AND RESCUE BEACON (SARBE) WITH TRANSCEIVER, 1960s

Receiver switch

Transmission switch

Battery

Transistor beacon

BRITISH EMERGENCY KIT, SUEZ CRISIS, 1956

Maps

"Blood chit" in English, Arabic, French, Greek, and other languages

Wire saw

Pouch

Booklet giving advice about local languages and customs

BRITISH ESCAPE BUTTON, 1990s

Button cover

Compass

Fishing line

BRITISH PACK OF FLARES, 1980s–1990s

Cover for flare

Lid

Fastener

Pack containing eight miniature flares

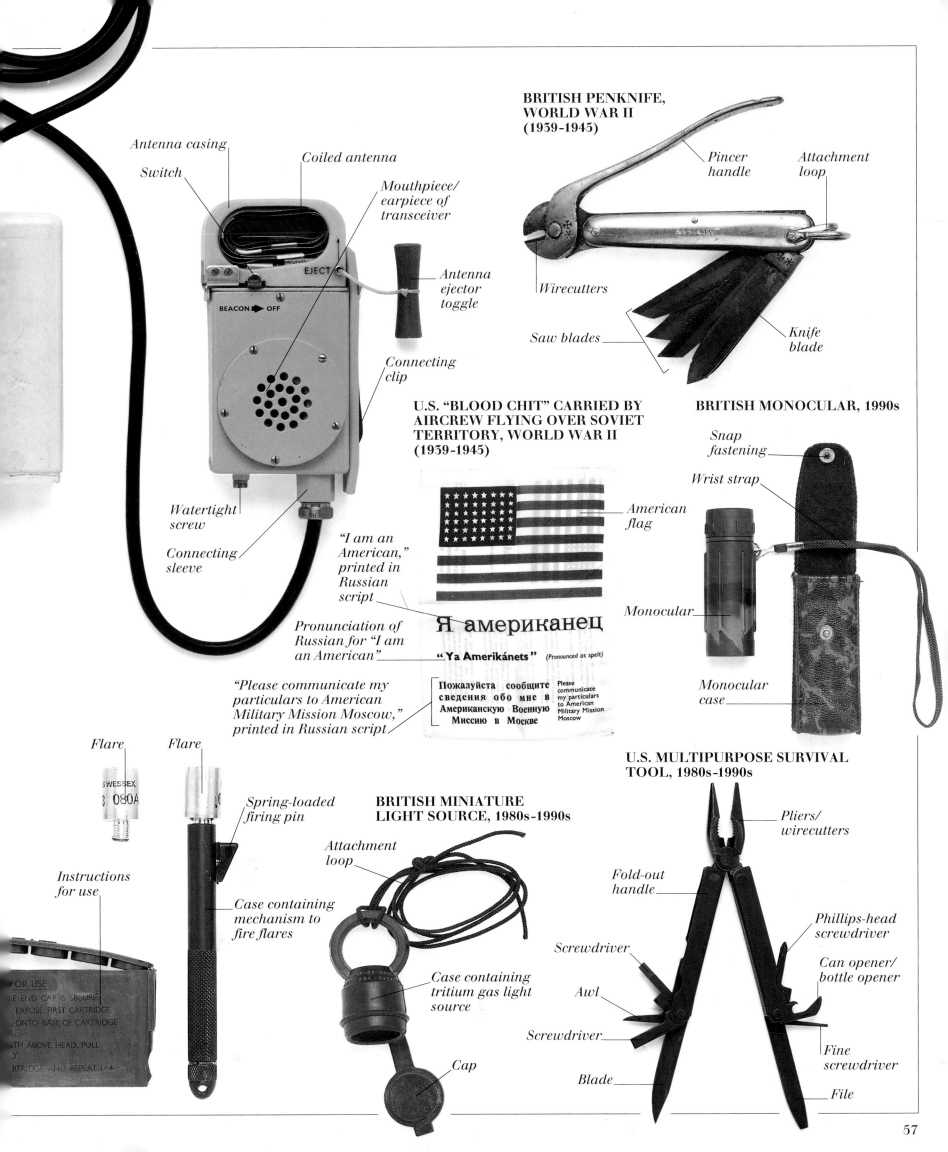

Antenna casing

Switch

Coiled antenna

**Mouthpiece/
earpiece of
transceiver**

**Antenna
ejector
toggle**

**Connecting
clip**

**Watertight
screw**

**Connecting
sleeve**

BRITISH PENKNIFE,
WORLD WAR II
(1939-1945)

**Pincer
handle**

**Attachment
loop**

Wirecutters

Saw blades

**Knife
blade**

U.S. "BLOOD CHIT" CARRIED BY
AIRCREW FLYING OVER SOVIET
TERRITORY, WORLD WAR II
(1939-1945)

BRITISH MONOCULAR, 1990s

**Snap
fastening**

Wrist strap

**American
flag**

Monocular

**Monocular
case**

**"I am an
American,"
printed in
Russian
script**

Я американец

"Ya Amerikánets" *(Pronounced as spelt)*

**Pronunciation of
Russian for "I am
an American"**

**"Please communicate my
particulars to American
Military Mission Moscow,"
printed in Russian script**

Пожалуйста сообщите
сведения обо мне в
Американскую Военную
Миссию в Москве

Please
communicate
my particulars
to American
Military Mission
Moscow

Flare

Flare

S WESSEX
080A

**Spring-loaded
firing pin**

**Attachment
loop**

BRITISH MINIATURE
LIGHT SOURCE, 1980s-1990s

U.S. MULTIPURPOSE SURVIVAL
TOOL, 1980s-1990s

**Pliers/
wirecutters**

**Fold-out
handle**

**Phillips-head
screwdriver**

**Can opener/
bottle opener**

Screwdriver

Awl

Screwdriver

**Fine
screwdriver**

Blade

File

**Instructions
for use**

FOR USE
E END CAP IS SECURE.
EXPOSE FIRST CARTRIDGE
ONTO BASE OF CARTRIDGE
TH ABOVE HEAD, PULL
Y.
RTRIDGE AND REPEAT 1-4

**Case containing
mechanism to
fire flares**

**Case containing
tritium gas light
source**

Cap

Escape and survival 2

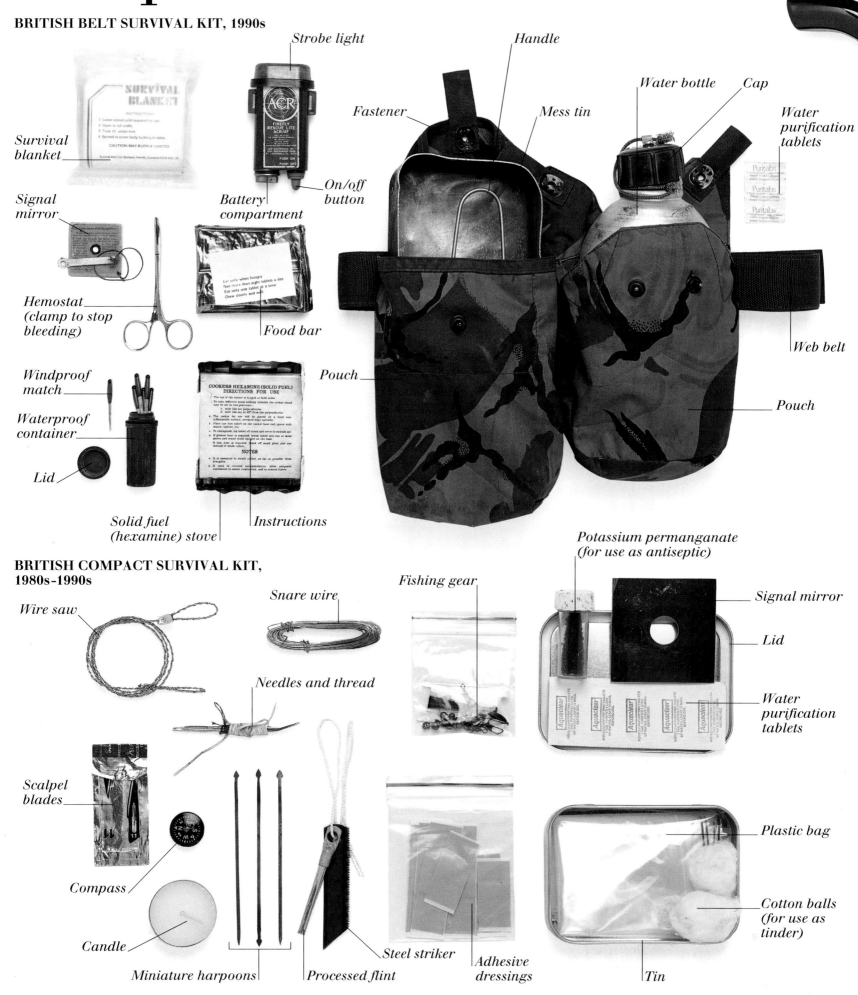

BRITISH BELT SURVIVAL KIT, 1990s

Survival blanket

Signal mirror

Strobe light

Battery compartment

On/off button

Hemostat (clamp to stop bleeding)

Food bar

Windproof match

Waterproof container

Lid

Solid fuel (hexamine) stove

Instructions

Fastener

Handle

Mess tin

Pouch

Water bottle

Cap

Water purification tablets

Web belt

Pouch

BRITISH COMPACT SURVIVAL KIT, 1980s–1990s

Wire saw

Snare wire

Fishing gear

Potassium permanganate (for use as antiseptic)

Signal mirror

Lid

Water purification tablets

Needles and thread

Scalpel blades

Compass

Candle

Miniature harpoons

Steel striker

Processed flint

Adhesive dressings

Plastic bag

Cotton balls (for use as tinder)

Tin

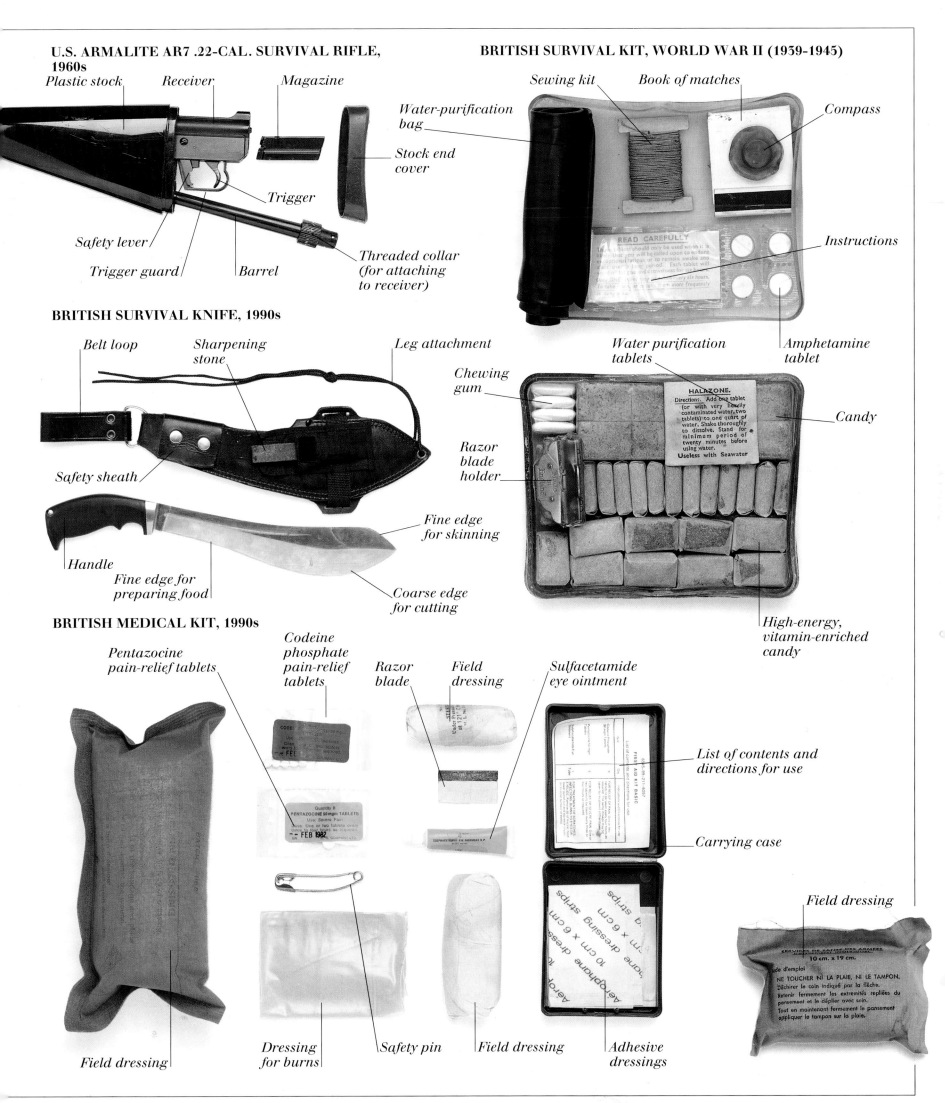

U.S. ARMALITE AR7 .22-CAL. SURVIVAL RIFLE, 1960s

Plastic stock
Receiver
Magazine
Stock end cover
Trigger
Safety lever
Trigger guard
Barrel
Threaded collar (for attaching to receiver)

BRITISH SURVIVAL KIT, WORLD WAR II (1939-1945)

Sewing kit
Book of matches
Water-purification bag
Compass
Instructions

READ CAREFULLY

Water purification tablets
Amphetamine tablet

BRITISH SURVIVAL KNIFE, 1990s

Belt loop
Sharpening stone
Leg attachment
Chewing gum
Candy
Safety sheath
Razor blade holder
Handle
Fine edge for preparing food
Fine edge for skinning
Coarse edge for cutting

HALAZONE.
Directions: Add one tablet (or with very heavily contaminated water, two tablets) to one quart of water. Shake thoroughly to dissolve. Stand for minimum period of twenty minutes before using water.
Useless with Seawater

High-energy, vitamin-enriched candy

BRITISH MEDICAL KIT, 1990s

Pentazocine pain-relief tablets
Codeine phosphate pain-relief tablets
Razor blade
Field dressing
Sulfacetamide eye ointment
List of contents and directions for use

FIRST AID KIT BASIC

Carrying case

Quantity 8
PENTAZOCINE 50mgm TABLETS
Use: Severe Pain
FEB 1982

Field dressing
Dressing for burns
Safety pin
Field dressing
Adhesive dressings
Field dressing

10 cm. x 19 cm.
NE TOUCHER NI LA PLAIE, NI LE TAMPON.

Index